W9-AQT-301

"The Journal is quite an undertaking—and a very worthy one! I like how the articles are tied together in the introduction and form a cohesive story. The Journal evolves from the components of donor relations and stewardship to the expansive review of the profession."

-**Ashleigh Manktelow**, Associate Director, Donor Relations, McGill University, Montréal, Québec

"With this first edition of the Journal of Donor Relations & Stewardship, *editors Julia Emlen and Anne Manner-McLarty have gathered some of the industry's top professionals to dive into a few of the most important topics for today's practitioners. By doing so, they are adding volume to the growing number of voices now proudly proclaiming the field to be deserving of academic study, treatment and discussion."*

-**Kay Coughlin**, Strategic Planner and Donor Experience Designer, Donor Relations Mindset, Columbus, Ohio

"Simply stated, all of the authors are brilliant. The depth of the material covered is top notch and each article builds upon points mentioned in the others. Reading The Journal makes me want to be a better writer. Overall, The Journal inspires personal responsibility for adding to the profession; I feel compelled to work to leave my shop better than I found it."

-**Paige Amick**, Director of Donor Relations and Stewardship, North Carolina A&T, Greensboro, North Carolina

"The Journal is a fascinating look at the fairly young profession of donor relations and stewardship. The article on professionalism makes you stop to think about a big topic we take for granted: the definition of a profession.

Philanthropy is evolving. The Journal overall makes compelling arguments that the time is now to elevate the donor relations function to a full-blown profession that is essential to the bottom line. "

"Congratulations on producing the Journal of Donor Relations & Stewardship*! You have certainly set the bar high on whatever follows in publications about our profession. Reading these articles makes me want to know more, to delve into even more specifics about our work."*

Journal of
Donor Relations
&Stewardship
Book 1: Definitions

Heurista Publications, LLC ©
1457 Merrimon Avenue • Asheville, NC 28804

www.JournalDRS.com

Publisher: Heurista Publications, LLC
Executive Editor: Julia Emlen
Managing Editor: Anne Manner-McLarty
Cover and Interior Design: Rachel McLarty

Printed in the United States of America
First Printing, 2016
ISBN 0-9974215-0-9
Library of Congress Control Number: 2016944460

Journal of Donor Relations & Stewardship
Book 1: Definitions

Contributors:

Erika R. Bernal, *MBA, CFRE, Senior Director of Development & Alumni Relations, Marshall B. Ketchum University*

Anne Manner-McLarty, *President and Lead Consultant, Heurista, Co.*

Daphne B. Powell, *Senior Director of Donor Relations and Stewardship, The University of Alabama at Birmingham*

Julia S. Emlen, *Principal, Julia S. Emlen Associates*

Nancy Lubich McKinney, *Executive Director of Donor and Gift Services, University of California, Berkeley*

Preface

When giving advice, Judith Martin, known in her writing and speaking as Miss Manners, addresses us as gentle readers. Hers is a kind and disciplined approach to rendering explanations about dealing with personal interactions. We admire Miss Manners, but we ask you to be fierce readers of this first volume of the *Journal of Donor Relations and Stewardship*. Those of us who have contributed to this journal and invested time, treasure and talent in its production want you to know that we are engaged in an enterprise to bring the conservation about our practice to a higher level. We want you to be engaged too.

The driving question in all our writing is *Why.* Why do we believe that what we do makes a difference in philanthropy? Why should something we are doing be considered a best practice? Why do we consider what we do a separate discipline in advancement? When we have asked ourselves why enough times, we can move to *How.* How do we determine that something we do has value in promoting giving to our organizations? How do we make sure that anything we do absorbs the fewest resources necessary to produce the greatest effect? Only when we have answered why and how can we proceed to *What.* We must clearly articulate the outcomes we are seeking and the ways in which we will measure our success before we focus on what we will do to bring our donors to their highest level of philanthropy.

In this first volume of the *Journal of Donor Relations and Stewardship*, we focus on definitions we use in our practice. Erika Bernal writes about compliance and examines the ethical and legal basis of the nonprofit enterprise. She considers the organizational and strategic factors that lay the groundwork for compliance management. She describes the ways in which practitioners work to assure that any donor's intentions are met while referencing the mission, vision, strategic direction and corporate policies and procedures of the organization.

Anne Manner-McLarty explores the landscape of recognition in all its manifestations. She examines how we can get recognition wrong when factors unrelated to appreciating a donor's contributions drive the recognition process. She makes recommendations that ensure an institutional recognition strategy underlies plans for donor appreciation and organizational advancement.

Erika's and Anne's articles discuss the fundamental components of stewardship and donor relations: compliance (stewardship); and recognition (donor relations). Our purpose in this first volume of the *Journal of Donor Relations and Stewardship* is to get to the basics of our practice, to give us definition of what we do. These two authors do just that.

Daphne Powell's article helps us understand one of the most important skills we use across our practice: writing. Expressing ourselves in words is critical to both donor relations and stewardship practice. Daphne defines types of writing and goes on to discuss how to identify good writers, interview and employ them, and train and provide continuing development opportunities for writers in donor relations and stewardship. She also talks about the resources available within an organization, such as style guides, that promote a consistent voice across the organization.

Julia Emlen writes about professionalism in donor relations and stewardship. Why do we consider ourselves professionals; how do we define our professional practice; how do we identify the aspects of professionalism in our practice; and what must we do to institutionalize and promote professionalism?

In this article, Julia picks up on topics discussed by Erika, Anne and Daphne. Erika's and Anne's articles fit into one of the definitions of professional practice promoted by Julia's piece, that of systems management professionalism. Both Erika and Anne describe practice that reaches across the organization, featuring collaboration with colleagues, coordination of assignments and production, dissemination of the mission, values, strategic direction and policy stance of the organization. These are the core of systems management professionalism. The recognition systems professional and the compliance systems professional anchor the practice of donor relations on the one hand and stewardship on the other. Daphne's article describes the work of another type of practitioner, the committed and competent professional, introduced in Julia's article.

The final presentation in this volume of the *Journal of Donor Relations and Stewardship* is an interview with Nancy Lubich McKinney about a definition vexing all of us: how does the structure of our shop compare to others. It is it large, small, somewhere in the middle; is it centralized or decentralized? How do we know? What difference does size or structure make in our effectiveness? Aside from helping us determine the conference workshops to attend when they are based on size or structure, this article helps us assess our working environment and determine the direction we might take depending on our goals. The article gives us a way to get the cart behind the horse, to see what modifications in our structure and resources might contribute to goal attainment. Resource development is not in itself a goal; it is a means of achieving goals.

Within this volume we've introduced a glossary of terms specific to the field of donor relations and stewardship. A far more extensive list is posted on our website and we invite our readers to comment and add to the list. This is important work as we continue to explore the why, how and what of our practice. We must begin with clarity about our work before we can advance our practice. Welcome to the conversation.

We invite our readers to enter into discussion with the editors, the authors and other practitioners through our website, journaldrs.com. We want to know what you think of the Journal of Donor Relations and Stewardship and of the ideas we have presented to you in this first volume. We encourage you to give us suggestions for additional articles. If you'll consider writing for the journal, we definitely want to hear from you.

We are particularly grateful to Heurista Publications staff members Ashleigh Hardes and Rachel McLarty, who have been the muscle in organizing this volume and our publication plan. Your eyes would not be taking in this journal without them. We appreciate the invaluable contribution of our final proof-reader, Paige Amick.

Thanks go out to our contributors as well: Erika Bernal, Daphne Powell and Nancy McKinney. These brave colleagues have produced thoughtful and thought-provoking articles. All three are skilled writers and professionals with long years of practice behind them. We are indebted to them for making the journal a reality.

We are grateful to a small group of colleagues and friends who took time from their busy professional lives to read the journal in manuscript. Their comments, corrections, suggestions and encouragement helped us complete the journal's first volume in record time. We salute commenters Anne Marie Halsey, Ashleigh Manktelow, Jack Fracasso, Rose Dalba, Mark Lanum, Kay Coughlin, Michal Shaw and Stephanie Mizer. We thank you all.

Julia S. Emlen, Executive Editor
Anne Manner-McLarty, Managing Editor

Glossary

Many of us haven't had any experience with glossaries since grammar school. We step back in time to introduce a glossary in the first volume of the *Journal of Donor Relations and Stewardship* to continue and support our efforts to regularize our practice through the use of common and accepted terms. We believe that having the glossary, and the conversation that we trust it will inspire, can revolutionize our practice through the common language we can use to discuss what we do.

We plan to develop a shared vocabulary of donor relations and stewardship over time and with participation from our audience. On our website, journaldrs.com, we have listed many words that we believe are important to our practice. We invite you to give us your thoughts on what these words and concepts mean in your practice. Furthermore, we encourage you to submit additional words, with or without definitions, to the glossary. As a community, we will develop new understanding and ready reference for the profession.

In addition, in each volume of the *Journal of Donor Relations and Stewardship*, we will select a number of words to feature. These words will be relevant for the topic covered by the journal. We will also call out a few words in each article that we believe are new terms for us to add to our professional lexicon.

This glossary does not supersede other glossaries of similar terms; it is not an attempt to be authoritative. We have assembled these words with these definitions to use in the *Journal of Donor Relations and Stewardship*. In these pages, this glossary pertains and we will use them consistently to allay confusion.

Donor Relations: The outcome of donor-based activities that seek to deliver the messages of the organization to philanthropists in order to attract and sustain their philanthropy for the realization of the mission of the organization. The instrument for assuring donor relations is recognition. A good donor relations outcome is an organizational priority, with all associated with the organization, from staff members through boards of directors, responsible for achieving consistency in delivering the messages of the organization. The recognition systems professional is responsible for coordinating institutional aspects of donor relations that may vary according to who the donor is, his/her relationship with the organization, and the significance of the donor and his/her philanthropy to the mission of the organization. The recognition systems professional also works across the organization to see that policies and procedures are in place to inform solicitation through training and message development so that philanthropists are recognized in various ways for their efforts to support the mission of the organization.

Stewardship: The outcome of gift-based activities that seek to build trust between philanthropists and the nonprofit organizations they may choose to support. The instrument for assuring stewardship is compliance and compliance management. A good stewardship outcome is an organizational priority, with all associated with the organization, from staff members through boards of directors, responsible for assuring the trustworthiness of the organization. The compliance systems professional is responsible for coordinating institutional aspects of stewardship that may vary according to the gift to assure the realization of donor intention. The compliance systems professional also works across the organization to see that policies and procedures of gift accounting and gift use are in place to inform solicitation through training and strategy development so that philanthropy is always supportive of the mission of the organization.

Fundraising: The raising of assets and resources from various sources for the support of an organization or a specific project.

Philanthropy: Philanthropy is defined in different ways. The origin of the word philanthropy is Greek and means love for mankind. Today, philanthropy includes the concept of voluntary giving by an individual or group to promote the common good. Philanthropy also commonly refers to grants of money given by foundations to nonprofit organizations. Philanthropy addresses the contribution of an individual or group to other organizations that in turn work for the causes of poverty or social problems improving the quality of life for all citizens. Philanthropic giving supports a variety of activities, including research, health, education, arts and culture, as well as alleviating poverty.

The Donor Bill of Rights: The text of the ten statements of the Donor Bill of Rights was developed by the American Association of Fund-Raising Counsel (AADRC), Association for Healthcare Philanthropy (AHP), Council for Advancement and Support of Education (CASE), and the Association of Fundraising Professionals (AFP) and adopted in November 1993. For purposes of the professional practice of donor relations and stewardship, the Donor Bill of Rights serves as a code of ethical practice. (See Appendix 1)

Beyond Compliance Basics: Results-Driven Stewardship

By Erika R. Bernal, MBA, CFRE

For nonprofit organizations, the many issues of compliance can be clouded by the desire to maintain a sparkling public image and by the organizational aspirations to do exceptionally clear and transparent work in the eyes of stakeholders. While these are two of the most laudable goals for nonprofits to achieve, they exist beyond the basics of what it takes to keep your nonprofit in compliance. We discuss in this article what nonprofit compliance is in general terms and what it is not. This is by no means an article that offers any sort of comprehensive legal counsel, but rather a discussion about building trust between nonprofits and their donors, and about delivering honorable results that promote the mission and vision of the nonprofit organization.

Nonprofit Compliance Basics

Those who seek to start a nonprofit organization from the ground up would learn the many ins and outs of nonprofit compliance laws related to establishing and maintaining nonprofit status. The laws are complex and change often[1]. Yet there are a few basic concepts to share as a basis for this discussion:

1. No shareholders and no promise of accrued dividends to shareholders.

    This is not to say that nonprofit organizations aren't deeply tied to a wide variety of stakeholders. Stakeholders will be defined for each nonprofit differently—they are our constituents, donors, patients, students, patrons, members, volunteers, employees and others. While nonprofits do not have the pressure of performing financially for shareholders, nonprofit performance is being increasingly scrutinized by all of our stakeholders, not forgetting the outside press and competing nonprofits.

2. No substantial profits on activities unrelated to the nonprofit's expressed mission. Furthermore, no substantial expenditure of time or money on unrelated activities.

While income is necessary to sustain the good work of the nonprofit, the nonprofit organization may not seek to generate significant means from activities beyond the core purpose of the organization nor spend excessive organizational time or money on the effort. These fundamental precepts ground each nonprofit in the vision and passion on which it was founded. This allows us as nonprofit leaders to think about ways in which our allocated time and resources can and should successfully advance our core purposes.

3. No lobbying to affect legislation in a substantial way.

Established within the definite confines of a legislative society, nonprofits by the nature of their work affect public perception and often seek to improve societal shortcomings otherwise not addressed by legislation. This results in an interesting paradigm, wherein our nonprofit organizations are challenged to influence change and deliver results through extraordinary action rather than by affecting law. Peter F. Drucker, famed management consultant and author, captures this relationship well, stating: "The 'nonprofit' institution neither supplies goods or services nor controls. Its 'product' is neither a pair of shoes nor an effective regulation. Its product is a changed human being."[2] As nonprofit organizations, we seek to deliver results that have an impact. As such we have the power to deliver solutions and inspire change in a very personal way.

4. No political campaign contributions.

This is pretty self-explanatory. Although, relating back to effectiveness of nonprofits to negotiate change for the greater good, our continuing contributions are those that influence the way that others operate on the most basic human level. We influence thought, action and emotion—to contribute politically as advocates of social justice, education, healthcare and the beauty in a creative, interconnected human world.

5. Keep exceptional records to defend against accusations of
    impropriety.

    In addition to a variety of other tax and financial requirements
    for maintaining nonprofit compliance, the rubber hits the road
    in the proper management of information and communication.
    Beyond the required annual return preparation, proper financial
    stewardship is a powerful tool to use in support of effectiveness as
    a nonprofit organization. Not the most glamorous, but good record-
    keeping is essential and the cornerstone of nonprofit compliance.

Compliance Affecting Daily Decisions and Output

In a 2013 blog post, Sue Gardner, special advisor to the Wikipedia
Foundation, captured a sentiment that is so fundamental to the
nonprofit community and yet in some offices still considered taboo—
revenue. Gardner shares, "Every nonprofit has two main jobs: you
need to do your core work, and you need the money to pay for it."[3]
Compared to the for-profit world, nonprofits rarely deliver tangible
product that can be bought and sold for revenue and ultimately
the sustainability of the organization. We operate in a world of
good feelings, righting societal wrong, aiding achievement for the
betterment of humankind. For the most part, nonprofits don't deliver
on effectiveness with increases in general sales performance and
higher gross revenue margins.

According to Gardner, however, it is clear that "Nonprofits also
prioritize revenue. But for most it doesn't actually serve as much of
an indicator of overall effectiveness." And this is her critical point,
"That's because donors rarely experience the core mission work first-
hand … over time many nonprofits have learned that the process of
giving needs—in and of itself—to provide a satisfying experience for
the donor." As a result, the core mission work that is touted in grant
proposals and face-to-face visits with donors becomes more of a goal,
an aspiration as opposed to an outcome.

How does this happen? In some respects, we lose sight of the
core mission. Our focus on delivering a timely IRS Form 990 or

minimizing costs related to dollars raised puts us in a never-ending administrative loop. Running giving reports that demonstrate activity and production in every way imaginable, delivering shiny marketing materials with smiling faces and passionate donor quotes, compiling donor reports that make each and every one of our contributors feel unique and special—these things all pull nonprofits away from our central mission work.

In the context of compliance, we build constraints around the need to deliver the positive and personal experiences for our donors. Consider the holy grail of recognition—accurate donor walls. Organizations may commit a full-time employee to the delivery of these precise public honor rolls. Standards, guidelines, even policies are put in place to ensure the fairness and timeliness of name placement and format. But when you really think about it, delivering a name on a paver or on an etched glass tile in the nonprofit hallway does not advance the typical nonprofit mission. Rather it adds a layer of administrative maintenance that can easily detract from the core mission work.

This is not to say that appropriate donor and volunteer recognition is not needed or useful. American psychologist Abraham Maslow would conclude that recognition is a need related to achieving *Esteem*— the fourth level in his popular framework describing the human hierarchy of needs. Esteem as a human motivation is placed beyond *Physiological, Safety, Love & Belonging*, and just before the fifth and highest human motivation of *Self-Actualization*.[4] Recognition itself falls in the lower of two categories of Esteem which satisfies the human need for respect from others; the higher category, as a matter of reference, is the need to respect one's self.

To an additional end, recognition provides that satisfying donor experience that Gardner describes so well, creating a sense of belonging to a donor community and encouraging future resource development as a result of donor commitment to our cause. Where the challenge remains is in the balance of achieving the mission in the midst of the administrative and remaining clear in the underlying goals of a process like updating a donor wall. Why do we do it? What is the desired end result? And are we able to afford resources, generated largely to achieve the core mission, on a process that can be both time and dollar demanding?

The unique answers to these questions will be based on the culture of the nonprofit organization and the extent to which a process like recognition enhances the donor experience and concurrently advances the mission. Critical thought should be put into anticipated return on effort; and institutions need to weigh effort against reward, making sure to define what "success" will ultimately mean for the project. The leanest organizations will eliminate traditional recognition activities, directing any revenue to the core mission. This approach provides the most opportunity to meet mission-critical goals with the full scope of resources available to do so. Other institutions may choose to deliver recognition by electronic devices as a cost-saving measure, and still others will continue the traditional print and public donor wall recognition. In all cases, it is essential to discuss thoroughly and consent to a shared approach for recognition that builds in a forward-thinking strategy for continued engagement. If the decision is made to spend the time and resources on recognition activity, then define and monitor the success of the effort. Build in measures of success and be willing to let a recognition practice go if your minimum level of return is not met, remembering, of course, that time and money spent on the donor reduces the amount of available resources for mission-critical efforts.

As dedicated professionals in a world where compliance dictates that we don't lobby, we can't spend undue time or resources on unrelated activity, and where we don't act and react for the benefit of any shareholder, we must stay committed to making sure that our efforts remain pure. Our demonstrated results as nonprofits affect real change to make the lives of countless individuals better by delivering the most basic human needs—food, water, health care, protection, education, family and artistic expression among many other things. To prioritize an administrative process such as recognition is by no means harmful; on the contrary, given the human desire to belong, it can incentivize great generosity. But it is not basic nonprofit compliance, and nonprofits can fall victim to fulfilling the donors' needs ahead of promoting the continuing needs of our core mission work.

The Proof Is in the Policy

Internal measures of compliance are often clarified with specific policy and procedure guidelines. By documenting these and sharing them publicly, a nonprofit is able to not only capture the critical thought and guiding processes within the organization, but it can also establish a framework to best set the expectations of individual donors. It is well understood that not all nonprofits are alike. As such, each institution must define for itself the lengths to which institutional resources should be spent on donor relations and stewardship initiatives, and each institution must be clear with donors what they can expect from the nonprofit in return.

Setting expectations begins with public policy documentation, defining which gifts are acceptable. Take time to analyze and document how your more unique gift types will be received. Record the process for accepting wire transfers, gifts of appreciated securities, charitable IRA contributions, deferred gifts, etc. Be realistic about what your organization can and cannot accept and thereafter steward effectively. Implement an annual review process for your major gift, stewardship and financial services officers to discuss policies and make any needed improvements from year to year. Inform your board and openly receive their feedback and expertise as engaged volunteers. After all, this level of transparency helps keep expectations manageable and sets your organization up for success.

Following a set of gift acceptance policies, record and implement a series of stewardship policies and recognition guidelines, capturing any public promises that your organization plans to make to donors in return for their generous giving. The key is consistency. Document plans for annual reporting, recognition and tax-related communication. Develop guidelines for which donors will receive special recognition, to what end and at which distinct levels of engagement. If you consider recognition as a tool to create interest and continued giving, define the minimum levels at which public recognition occurs and the maximum levels of organizational spending related to public recognition. Remember that the effective nonprofit curbs substantial expenditures of time or money to ensure that donor dollars are being spent to the fullest extent possible on core mission work.

At minimum, end with a solid process for capturing donor intent on significant gifts. Once again "significant" can mean very different things across organizations, ranging anywhere on the low end from $1,000 to $100,000. Whatever the level, it is important to record donor intent accurately and succinctly so that those who steward the donor have a clear sense of the deliverables. As donor relations and stewardship professionals create personalized plans for donor stewardship, clear communication between donor, gift officer and stewardship officer is mandatory to maintain the highest levels of accuracy and deliverability. When gift agreements are too restrictive, both the donor and the institution suffer. Understand your organization's needs, communicate clearly to the donor and work openly with the donor to put dollars to use for the best program possible. While it is difficult to turn down a gift that is overly restrictive, be willing and available to do so. Avoid gifts to specific individuals—such as researchers, department chairs, physicians—as employment circumstances may change and the institution is left with overly restricted funds. Remember that you are both an agent of the institution and also an advocate for your donor when he or she cannot be present. You are uniquely positioned to identify the best collaborative end, and your gift agreement process should capture those ends clearly for all restricted gifts, endowed and current use.

Gift agreements and statements of gift intent can be enforceable in the court if written properly. However, the hope is that by managing expectations well, donors will remain committed to the institution's mission, satisfied with the use of the gifted dollars and engaged on a much deeper level with the core work being done. It is that core mission that drew them to you in the first place. Make good on your commitments by being clear and upfront throughout the gift and stewardship process.

Real Impact at Real Costs

Diving deeper into the area of cost over impact, we turn to major influencers in the area of study, such as David Greco, managing director of Social Sector Partners and lead project director for the Real Cost Project. In a recent forum designed to bring nonprofits together with charitable funders to discuss areas of efficiency and need, Greco spoke to hundreds of leaders representing Orange County, Calif. nonprofits and grantors about the efficiencies of grant-making and grant-asking in a nonprofit world that has changed dramatically in recent years. Titled "Real Costs. Real Outcomes." Greco's presentation inspired critical thought about the cost versus impact relationship.[5]

Simple in approach, the Real Cost Project[6] is an effort started by California grantors seeking to define real cost and administer grant funds based on real cost funding to achieve higher level results. Through open conversation with nonprofits, the Real Cost Project starts with effective outcomes in mind and seeks to better understand the program costs, operating costs and reserve/capital costs needed for effective program delivery and sustainability. The Real Cost Project concurs with the premise of this earlier discussion, "Like any enterprise—including for-profit corporations—nonprofits must be able to cover the real cost of their programs and operations if they are to deliver excellent outcomes."

Whether for major grantors or individual donors, the basis of effective and meaningful stewardship reporting is understanding basic nonprofit needs as well as the role that donors play in meeting these needs and achieving better results. For trust-building to begin, honest and honorable outcomes must be communicated effectively. As nonprofits, we should feel confident approaching our funders with reports on real costs. It takes people to do good work (salary and program management costs), and trial and error to reach efficient ends (research and evaluation costs). To deliver better results, nonprofits must be cognizant of exactly how donor dollars are being spent. This notion is central to nonprofit compliance efforts to keep costs closely tied to the expressed mission and organizational objectives.

Often, in an effort to report big results and incredible impact, nonprofits feel pressured to stay vague and report broadly. This approach seeks to deliver on the continuing need for a positive donor experience by keeping impact results teetering at unsustainable levels, nevertheless they are levels that impress our donors and inspire them to give again. Perhaps it would be more strategic to impress them with real project numbers, to bring them into the organizational folds by explaining exactly how their dollar helps, and to help them realize how each dollar is contributing to the overall solution.

To report impact from a cost perspective, nonprofits will need to drill down into their spending and budgeting patterns. In today's world, funders are trying to give "smarter" by allocating resources to winning programs. While federal funding continues to decline and at the same time social markets demonstrate growing need for support, members of the philanthropic community will seek to leverage their dollars to achieve better results. In this instance, nonprofits need to innovate and evolve to meet the rising expectations of donors. The payoff, however, is that today's sophisticated donor seeks to invest in innovation. There exists a definite win-win if nonprofits build the trust and deliver on their promise to achieve maximum impact at an efficient cost.

In its 2015 State of the Nonprofit Sector report,[7] the Nonprofit Finance Fund compiled survey results from nonprofits across the U.S. on their financial health and management strategies. It is an ongoing nationwide effort that, in their words, seeks to use data to spark dialogue in service to change. Among their findings:

- Of those nonprofits surveyed, 76% projected that their service and/ or program demand slightly or significantly increased in 2014; and less than 4% of respondents reported any measure of decrease in demand

- Of these, less than half (48%) reported being able to meet the increased demand in 2014, with 71% of respondents reporting that client needs remain unmet without their services

- 78% of nonprofits surveyed reported 6 months or less of cash readily available; and a staggering 53% reported less than 3 months of cash-on-hand

- The top three reported greatest challenges: achieving long-term financial sustainability (32%); offering competitive pay and/or retaining staff (25%); and raising funding that covers full costs (19%)

By every measure, nonprofits are demonstrating incredible need for further funding. It is not proof of financial burden that donors seek, but rather proof of efficiency and innovative action to deliver results. We are challenged to reduce waste in expenditures, focus on the mission and in so doing influence process changes to streamline program efforts, all the while delivering better results to more people in need. No matter what your mission entails, this is a tall order.

The Murky Mission

Thinking about truth in reporting, we must discuss what happens in the donor relations and stewardship departments when the mission of the organization gets clouded. This may happen as a result of a highly prescriptive donor or volunteer, overly restrictive gift agreements, aggressive gift acceptance processes that don't clearly define expectations or simply because of a change in structure of a nonprofit institution. When the mission isn't clear, it is impossible to manage donor expectations properly and deliver results that more deeply engage your donors.

The lack of clarity can create anxiety. Program directors don't know how best to spend dollars; donors often expect results that are either unrealistic or outside the normal scope of deliverables; stewardship officers find work-around processes for measuring impact and managing reports. Without a clear mission, the nonprofit loses its ability to operate efficiently and adds both cost and time to administrative functions. When the mission doesn't remain the most central aspect of your fundraising process, you segment efforts and often weaken operations.

This is not to say a strict tunnel-focus is required to do good work. It is through change and trials that innovative approaches develop. There exist donors who seek to take organizations to new levels, and their contributions demand creative thought and new process developments. It is wise to recognize these situations and define them for what they are—outside core mission work. Perhaps a special team is assigned to manage follow-through and measure success. Or perhaps a workflow process is devised to streamline efforts and bring work processes back into the fold. Thought and planning on the front end, coupled with clear measurements for success help the nonprofit to avoid the pitfalls that develop when new processes are in constant demand due to change and lack of clarity. By doing so, the nonprofit minimizes nonessential activity, keeps the core mission work in mind and keeps costs lower by maintaining efficiency in planning and operations.

Standards for Nonprofit Evaluation

To discuss proper stewardship and cost-based impact without a section on evolving standards for nonprofit evaluation would be incomplete. Let's begin with the costs associated with overhead or operating expenses for organizations set up to be sustained by charitable gifts rather than profits. As part of the annual IRS Form 990 filing, nonprofits must report program, administrative and fundraising expenses separately—the latter two combined making up the operating expenses or overhead support for the year.[8] The notion behind such directive disclosures by the IRS is to share openly with the public exactly how nonprofits spend their money.

Historically, it is assumed that the lower the overhead, the more effective the nonprofit. But to be clear, the IRS does not establish any sort of evaluative equation or appropriate level of spending in each of these categories. The goal is simply transparency. General expectations for low operating expenses have developed from third-party rating systems that charities rely on for public approval. It might be completely reasonable for a nonprofit to spend up to 40% on operating costs to ensure fair pay for employees, suitable office space, upgraded computer systems and databases, not to mention proper training;

however, higher marks on charity rating sites for lower overhead costs influence nonprofits to minimize necessary expenditures on resource and staff development. As a result, nonprofits on average offer lower salaries, keep staff counts to a minimum, potentially overworking their employees and, in the worst occasions, develop reputations for ineffective processes and/or depressed working conditions.

Certainly, these conditions are not always the reality. The Overhead Myth—a website created by leaders of the Better Business Bureau Wise Giving Alliance, GuideStar USA and Charity Navigator—shares an open letter to donors to correct misconceptions that overhead ratios accurately and independently measure charity performance.[9] This is evidence of a systematic overhaul taking shape. While ironic in that the charity rating systems themselves contributed to the myth, in their letter, the CEOs of all three aforementioned charity rating agencies petition donors to consider the broader impact of the nonprofit's work by stating, "We ask you to pay attention to other factors of nonprofit performance: transparency, governance, leadership, and results." They even go so far as to encourage higher overhead costs for nonprofits by detailing, "Overhead costs include important investments charities make to improve their work: investments in training, planning, evaluation, and internal systems—as well as their efforts to raise money so they can operate their programs."

The Overhead Myth details statistics about the use of overhead ratios in nonprofit evaluation, citing eye-opening figures about the imprecision and inaccuracy in overhead reporting. Among them:

- 37% of nonprofit organizations with private contributions of $50,000 or more reported no fundraising or special event costs

- 13% of operating public charities reported spending nothing for management and general expenses

- 75-85% of these organizations were incorrectly reporting the costs associated with grants

What has resulted is a biased consumer- or donor-driven model for nonprofit evaluation. In survey results from 2001, BBB Wise Giving

Alliance found that more than half of American adults thought that nonprofits should operate with a 20% overhead rate or less. Furthermore, these same survey respondents placed overhead ratio and financial transparency above demonstrated success when evaluating their willingness to give. As nonprofits, we clearly hope this perception has changed or at the least has begun to change given recent efforts.

This is an unrealistic approach to nonprofit evaluation. Fortunately, the tenacity to change perception and to implement results-driven reporting has already led to more progressive nonprofit models that have taken good programs to levels of greatness. As nonprofits, these are our fiercest competitors for funding and our would-be mentors if we were smart about it. The nonprofits that put mission above all else capitalize on the human power to make a difference. They create environments for their employees that stimulate and inspire good work. They take their donors on a journey of success because people have been helped and resources shared to better the situation of someone less fortunate.

What begins as a matter of compliance by filing that IRS Form 990 results once again in the honorable intentions of nonprofits being muddied by the critique of public perception. Ensure that your nonprofit organization stays above the fray by delivering on your promise to the community around you—to those you serve and to those you engage to fund your programs. We should all find ways to allocate our limited time and resources in ways that can successfully advance our core purposes.

Getting Beyond the Basics

As perceptions of nonprofit success evolve, there is nothing but incredible opportunity to work directly with your key stakeholders, funders, nonprofit partners and internal evaluators to ensure that you achieve the delivery of real results measured effectively against your mission. Talk to each other openly about the needs of your nonprofit and find areas of commonality where your donors expect to use their dollars to further the good work of your organization. Not all donors are alike. While one may give regularly and often to the most universal pressing needs of the organization, another may prefer taking a program of interest to the next level with a one-time influx of capital. Both of these donors are critical to managing the way forward.

After the Sarbanes-Oxley (SOX) legislation[10] was passed by Congress in 2002—in response to multiple for-profit scandals involving Enron, WorldCom, and Arthur Anderson among others—nonprofits scurried to implement policies and procedures that did not all technically apply to them. In fact, some of the most critical new mandates of the SOX legislation were already common practice in nonprofits. The fraud, unethical compensation practices, and widespread conflicts of interest tied to the offending for-profit corporations ripped a gaping hole in the trust of Americans. We still suffer from levels of mistrust today, misuse of power and misuse of donor dollars. But the takeaway is that we can all be better at what we do because of results-driven reporting and cost-based evaluation. We can all be better at what we do because those who are deeply engaged with our mission call on us to deliver results.

So let's not disappoint. We recognize that all nonprofits depend on maintaining trust and donor loyalty to raise funds and continually enhance our public image. To be mired in nonessential administrative tasks consumes our availability to think, work, learn and do all things mission-centric. Give yourself, as nonprofits leaders, the time to critically evaluate your approach. And identify where you can make process changes, resource investments and creative improvements to accomplish your end goal and make a lasting impact on the life of someone else in need.

Erika R. Bernal, MBA, CFRE, is the senior director of development & alumni relations at Marshall B. Ketchum University. Erika has held a series of development and donor relations positions in healthcare and higher educational institutions in Southern California and has served as an executive officer and board director of the Association of Donor Relations Professionals.

Endnotes

[1] "Tax Information for Charities & Other Nonprofits." *IRS.gov*, accessed March 21, 2016, www.irs.gov/Charities-&-Non-Profits.

[2] Peter F. Drucker, *Managing the Nonprofit Organization: Principles and Practices*. HarperCollins, 1990.

[3] Sue Gardner, "What's *Really* Wrong with Nonprofits—And How We Can Fix It," *Sue Gardner's Blog*. Last modified October 20, 2013. http://suegardner. org/2013/10/20/whats-really- wrong-with- nonprofits-and- how-we-can-fix- it/

[4] Abraham H. Maslow, "A Theory of Human Motivation," *Psychological Review* 50, no. 4 (1943): 370-96.

[5] David Greco, "Real Costs. Real Outcomes." (presentation, Orange County Funders Roundtable, Anaheim, CA, February 4-5, 2016).

[6] "The Real Cost Project." *Real Cost Project - A Project of Northern California Grantmakers in collaboration with San Diego Grantmakers and Southern California Grantmakers*, accessed March 21, 2016, www.realcostproject.org.

[7] "2015 State of the Nonprofit Sector Survey: National Results (May 2015)." *Nonprofit Finance Fund*, accessed Mach 21, 2016, www.nonprofitfinancefund.org/ sites/default/files/docs/2015/2015survey_natl_full_results.pdf.

[8] "Current Form 990 Series - Forms and Instructions." *IRS.gov*, accessed March 21, 2016, www.irs.gov/uac/Current-Form-990- Series-Forms- and-Instructions.

[9] "Moving Toward an Overhead Solution." *The Overhead Myth*, accessed March 21, 2016,www.overheadmyth.com.

[10] "A Guide to the Sarbanes-Oxley Act." Sarbanes-Oxley Act 2002, accessed March 21, 2016, www.soxlaw.com.

A Call for Donor Recognition Strategy

By Anne Manner-McLarty

Strategic management of donor recognition is a hallmark of a fully mature approach to donor relations and stewardship. This article reviews the broad array of activities that fall under the heading "donor recognition" and addresses how the categories of donor recognition best align with organizational goals. It demonstrates how strategically planned donor recognition can benefit donor relations and stewardship, calls into question common practices and prepares the reader to better evaluate recent trends. The article includes tools for recognition program management, including preparing for change within the program over time.

Content

- Clarifying the range and purposes of donor recognition
- Establishing strategic goals for donor recognition
- Building a donor recognition program
- Developing standard program documentation
- Analyzing return on investment for donor recognition

Glossary

- Donor recognition: Any activity or item used by an organization to express appreciation to or for those who provide philanthropic support to the organization. Better examples communicate to the public the value placed on philanthropy by the organization, demonstrate an awareness of the individuality of the relationship to the donor and celebrate the donor's role in the organization's ability to meet its mission.

- Recognition program: A strategic model for creating recognition outcomes—messages, activities and product solutions—that can be applied to an unlimited variety of situations. A successful recognition program balances recognition for different types of giving, involves internal and external stakeholders efficiently, anticipates changes in donor volume, brand messaging, architecture and technology and ultimately contributes to increased giving. A recognition program is different from even the most comprehensive set of donor recognition product solutions in that it promotes problem-solving in the face of new circumstances.

- Policy: a course or set of principles adopted by a government, party, business, organization or individual
- Strategy: a plan of action designed to achieve a major or overall aim
- Tactic: a carefully planned action taken to accomplish a specific aim; an individual action or practice that supports a strategy
- Procedure: an established or official way of carrying out a task; a series of actions conducted in a certain order or manner

Why Donor Recognition Matters

As a consultant, I have had the good fortune to see organizations of many sizes and types in action. I am inspired by the work these organizations do, yet I'm often dismayed by how poorly they manage their donor recognition practices. When it comes to donor recognition, strategy seems to be lacking at most fundraising organizations. I mean there is no specific process for creating and working a plan, measuring the success of those efforts and revising the plan in order to achieve perpetual excellence. Instead, tradition, convenience, budget, the opinion of a person in a position of authority or donor preference seem to drive donor recognition decision-making. Priorities seem arbitrary and there are missed opportunities to enhance the recognition experience for the donors, advance the broader storytelling potential of donor recognition and maximize the return on investment for the organization.

Strategizing human relationships—especially in terms of generosity and gratitude—can seem artificial or manipulative, yet how is it really different from fundraising strategy? Our donors make gifts because they expect an outcome tied to the mission of the organization. If strategizing donor recognition helps the organization realize its mission, would not the donor be proud to know that a strategy is in place?

Recognition is understood as a reaction to giving. It is treated as a decision to be made and executed after the gift has been received and is largely driven by an organization's sense of obligation to the donor.

"It's the right thing to do" is the primary logic regarding investment in donor recognition. Pleasing donors becomes the motivating force and too little thought goes into making the experience appropriate to the character of the organization. Recognition is rarely part of a strategy to create greater affinity between the donor and the organization or to motivate giving at the donor's highest potential. There are vague claims about the public nature of recognition contributing to giving by others, but little effort goes into maximizing that potential. At most organizations, donor recognition has no specific goals and few measures of success.

> *Donor recognition must become more than a response to a gift or a response to a notification of an intended gift. In its purest form, donor recognition is a strategic tool for communicating with current and prospective donors. At its most genteel, it's a thoughtful relationship with your best friends. The methods of your stewardship program and the activities you perform in thanking those who fund your mission are the keys to enhanced giving, both now and in the future.[1]*

Leading professionals agree that recognition is one of the four principles of good stewardship practice.[2] Those principles are:

1. Meticulous gift acceptance practices leading to timely and accurate acknowledgment

2. Impact reporting to bring the donor closer to the organization through honest data and effective storytelling

3. Recognition

4. Ongoing engagement to encourage the donor to become an advocate for the organization and to make a next gift

Recognition has its own distinct functions within the practice of donor relations and stewardship. Recognition is a celebration of the organization's relationship to a particular donor and to philanthropy in general. It is as much about the organization formulating its response to generosity as it is about expressing gratitude to the donor. The word "recognition" comes from the Latin verb *recognoscere* meaning "to know again or recall to mind." Our industry's definition of recognition, "to show official appreciation of or formally reward" appears further down the list of possible meanings.[3] The two definitions point to the dual purposes of all public recognition: to demonstrate to the donor an awareness of the individuality of his or her contribution, often while communicating to the public at large—donors and potential donors alike—the value placed on philanthropy and the donor's role in the organization's ability to meet its mission.

All donor recognition should perform the following functions:

1. Communicate the critical relationship between philanthropic support and the organization's ability to meet its mission.

2. Represent the voice of the organization with specificity and authenticity.

3. Acknowledge the specific nature of the giving from the donor or group of donors listed.

4. Accurately identify the donor or donors.

5. Demonstrate gratitude for the organization's philanthropic supporters.

The priority and balance of the these functions will vary based on the size and type of organization, the complexity of the donor relationships managed and the specific goals assigned to the donor recognition activities.

Clarifying Terms

There is a puzzling lack of clarity about what constitutes donor recognition. Today my work addresses the full spectrum of donor relations and stewardship practice. Early in my career, however, I focused solely on the design of donor recognition displays and plaques that hung on the walls of my clients' buildings. I trained with leaders in the industry who taught me the benefits of investing in materials of the highest quality, architectural integration and program planning. I bought into the notion that investing in strategy and design would result in stronger philanthropy.

Through this work, I came to realize that the term donor recognition describes many different things. The scope of "donor recognition" is dizzyingly broad. Recognition can mean a letter; an event; items given to donors as tokens of appreciation; or any variety of donor listings, including formal naming of spaces, programs, faculty positions and scholarships. With the advent of digital media, donor walls can include electronic displays or be expressed as virtual experiences on a website. Only occasionally does the term donor recognition refer to an item with one or more donor names on it. To further complicate things, each type of giving program warrants a different approach. To design donor recognition, we must negotiate the details of annual, cumulative, consecutive, capital, or planned giving programs or navigate the complexities of a group of individual gifts resulting in a set of naming opportunities.

With experience, I've come to understand recognition as a practice, not a single activity or item. I now appreciate recognition as one among many of an organization's donor relations and stewardship responsibilities and have come to accept that it can take many forms.

Questioning Basic Donor Recognition Concepts

In our field, donor recognition is sometimes loosely defined as "parties, pins and plaques." In other words, recognition is any of a variety of activities or objects used to show appreciation of a donor, both publicly and privately. The problem is that many people assume that all types of donor recognition are effectively equal and that personal preference, opinion or industry trends are effective means of choosing which methods to employ.

Settling into easy-to-achieve outcomes, habits and so-called norms to guide recognition practice results from a desire for predictable routine, efficiency and consistency. There's a bit of laziness in this approach. If what was done last year seemed to suffice, it can be done again. If what the institution across town is doing is working, it must be a common practice worth emulating. If the donor says he or she is happy, we trust that it is so and are pleased to apply the same logic to the next donor. We don't take the time to define our goals and compare our assumptions against the needs and behaviors specific to the organization and its donor community.

This lack of specificity has contributed to an assumption that any one of the donor recognition activities is as useful as the others, that they are, in fact, *interchangeable*. Some practitioners erroneously believe a letter will substitute for a face-to-face conversation and a plaque might be a reasonable alternative to a gathering of people sharing similar interests and motivations.

Donor recognition tactics are usually structured around the type of gift and the gift amount. This structure is quickly adopted because it makes donor recognition planning easier. It becomes predictable. Predictability, however, can undermine the genuine connection between the donor and the mission of the organization. A *predictable* pattern of action is a worthwhile goal, yet a predictable outcome will likely be seen as generic or cliché.

Organizations regularly default to *nonspecific* recognition out of necessity. The staff person developing the recognition content has too little access to specific detail or too many stories to develop. As a result, we see lists without context, vague references to donor history and generalization about donor impact. Most plaques are a brief historical record, lacking any true recognition of the person listed. Lists are forgotten with the next magazine or annual report except in the anxiety they produce among those who compile them.

Any donor recognition activity—letter, event, memento or listing—most often happens on a schedule *convenient* for the organization's staff. Recognition activities are usually planned around fundraising, construction and administrative schedules. Rarely are they aligned with the donor's emotions after having made a significant gift. The duration of the modern fundraising campaign forces major contributors to wait years for the completion of the buildings or initiatives that have been promised as recognition opportunities. Doesn't it make sense that a donor's delight wanes when it takes so long for a naming opportunity to come to fruition? Lengthy campaigns increase the need for recognition strategy that provides timely and perhaps frequent opportunities for donor recognition.

Focusing on the program structure without pushing for meaningful, donor-centered content will result in recognition outcomes that are interchangeable, predictable, nonspecific and convenient. This approach flattens the donor recognition process and defeats strategy, even though it looks like a well-devised plan. It substitutes structure for meaning resulting in a generic outcome with less than optimal impact on the very donors it is meant to influence.

The Case for Strategy

Strategic planning establishes a specific set of goals that are aligned with the mission of the organization. The goals are lofty and future focused. Some goals are the same for all organizations, yet the strategies for achieving them are different for each organization and change over time. Strategies are typically aligned with a larger vision that affects all organizational planning, not just the fundraising effort. They should be clearly stated and available to everyone within the organization. They are the basis for donor recognition tactics, the activities carried out over time.

Most donor recognition happens at the tactical level. Donor recognition is most effective when it is clearly aligned with larger organizational strategy.

As donor relations professionals, we have obligations to both our donors and the organizations we represent. It is our job to be the conduit for those relationships and in managing them, in stewarding them and helping them grow and evolve, we must employ strategy. We must ask, what does the donor need from this relationship in order to feel appreciated for his or her unique contribution at the same time we ask what does the organization require and how is that best accomplished?

All fundraising organizations need to bring donors to their highest level of philanthropy within the scope of their relationship to the organization and its specific mission. In other words, all donor recognition should motivate greater giving from existing donors. Every donor recognition practice must include strategy to move donors to give again.

All organizations share the need to engage new donors. Donor recognition has the unique ability to demonstrate the value the organization places on philanthropy in general and the individual donor in particular. The emotional nature of donor recognition is inherently powerful. For that reason, all donor recognition should maximize its impact on all audiences, assuming they are all potential donors. It should be designed to entice new donors into the joy of giving and the specific satisfaction of realizing this organization's mission.

All organizations need to communicate a unique and specific ability to accomplish their missions. Recognizing donor support, especially in a public forum, is an outlet for restating the mission, celebrating accomplishments and honoring the donor's role in those achievements. Strategy must ensure the donor is recognized as an individual having made a winning decision and seen as endorsing the organization.

Other strategies will depend on the specifics of the organization. The mission will direct strategy. A campaign will drive strategy. The strengths or particular vision of leadership will influence strategy. It is imperative that those charged with developing donor recognition strategy be familiar with these larger goals and the tools and tactics being used by other units or departments. By aligning with tactics in other areas of the organization, the outcomes become more specific and more meaningful to the donor. The donor feels that he or she is engaged with the whole organization, not just the fundraising effort or the individual assigned to donor recognition.

Strategies change slowly. Most often they are reviewed annually and are modified over time in a pattern that reflects changes at the institutional level. Tactics, however, may change more often, depending on their purpose, frequency of use and the number of times that a given donor will be engaged using the same tactic.

Building a Donor Recognition Program

With strategic objectives established, it is easier to sort through the different types of donor recognition and make tactical choices that align with those goals. Decisions about how many events to hold in a year and what format they should take are based on estimated return on investment. The details of what type of donor recognition display to purchase, how much to pay for it, where to put it and who to list on it are far less daunting when there is clarity about the reasons for having a display at all. Best yet, the impetus to follow the latest trend dissipates and checking strategic goals and confirming that each tactic meets the needs of both the organization and the donor becomes standard practice.

Managing Donor-Centricity in Recognition Practice

I often hear a certain rubric in planning any donor relations activity: is it good for the donor? While this is an important question to ask, in the case of donor recognition, it is not the only factor to be considered. We must commit to doing better than is required in service to the donor, the organization and the mission when planning donor recognition strategy.

I also hear advice that suggests that the details of the donor recognition strategy won't matter as long as the donor is pleased. Organizations misinterpret the concept of "donor-centered" and establish subjective goals like "surprising and delighting" donors as a measure of success. While it is laudable to excel in the expression of gratitude, setting this as a goal is not a substitute for a fully actuated donor recognition strategy. One must understand the objectives of various recognition activities, beyond pleasing the donor, and strive to achieve the greatest effect with the time and money invested in donor recognition.

At the other extreme, public recognition is sometimes omitted at the request of a donor with very little debate from the organization about the loss from having done so. Private activities may take place; but publicly, it is as if the gift never happened. Future philanthropy from this donor and others may suffer. Worse yet, the opportunity to tell an important story, one that has the same potential as any other to motivate giving, is lost. Unless the donor requests complete anonymity and no public mention of the gift, the organization must also consider the need to support the mission through recognition and negotiate a donor-approved way to tell an anonymous story.

At higher giving levels, most organizations create recognition activities that appeal to the particular interests of the individual donor. This often includes more exclusive access and information, which is relatively private and takes advantage of the immediate circumstances. When recognition takes a permanent place in the organization's facilities, however, strategy must focus first on design standards and content guidelines. The outcome must address the audience that will see it every day even more than the donor who may see it only once. Thoughtfully planned, the experience for the donor is in the development of the story and the legacy building it provides. The event planned around the plaque or display should be more meaningful to the donor than the product itself. Be cautious about setting precedents that cannot be maintained for other donors presenting similar circumstances.

In all situations, the donor's wishes must be considered concerning privacy, perhaps up to and including anonymity. Most organizations have established systems for tracking donor requests for anonymity which may mean no public recognition, no recognition outside a limited circle of people, no recognition until a certain time, or in rare cases, no communication about the gift at all.

Determining Best Applications for Various Types of Donor Recognition

Most organizations must build a donor recognition program with limited resources of staff time and dollars. To that end, the same concepts that apply to creating sustainable acknowledgment and reporting practices will guide donor recognition planning. With so many options for donor recognition activities, it is important to plan with efficiency and specific goals in mind.

1. Mass communication, with personalization whenever possible, is the building block for any donor recognition program.

2. More customized communications, such as individually crafted letters and phone calls, are the next component developed by most organizations.

3. When appropriate, tours or meetings with leaders, researchers or service providers are a good first step for top donors.

4. Events, large or small, can serve as important networking and information sharing opportunities.

When we clarify the purpose of the various recognition activities, it is apparent that each has a unique role in overall stewardship strategy. The tactical requirements of each type of recognition become more obvious, too.

These are examples of general tactics:

1. A letter or phone call is a good way to establish or continue the personal connection between the organization and the donor. This type of communication is best delivered or carried out in a timely fashion, relating to the date of the gift or the timing of an update on project progress.

2. Meetings and tours are a sign of inclusion and can be structured to enhance the sense of behind-the-scenes access. Donor recognition tactics might include time for the donors to meet with scholarship students, a case manager, researcher or the organization's leadership.

3. Most events with multiple donors, even the largest ones, are about networking, sometimes with those responsible for service delivery, sometimes with beneficiaries. In every case, there is an important aspect of gathering with other donors. The event must be structured to foster interactions.

4. Permanent public recognition like displays or plaques have a long lifespan and a broad audience. These tools should be designed to have meaning for all audiences. The donor experience can be enhanced through the planning of an unveiling event and photos or other tangible items for the donor to take away from the event.

Donor recognition activities can be private or public, ephemeral or permanent and reside at the organization or with the donor. We must consider each activity as it is planned, making choices that align with strategy. As needed, establish schedules for rejuvenation of the program components to keep those that a donor might encounter multiple times fresh and topical.

Figure 1: Types of donor recognition by intended purpose, audience and outcome

Activity	Method	Audience	Destination	Permanence	Legacy Building Potential
Thank you letter	Mailed, emailed or hand delivered	Donor, anyone with whom the donor shares it and the donor record	Donor's personal files and donor record held by the organization	Unknown with donor; public record of the organization	Historical record; improved with the level of detail within the letter
A meeting with a key faculty member or service provider	Scheduled on site or at an agreed location	Attendees only	Semi-private	Temporal; recorded in varying detail	Improved personal relationships
Multiple-donor event, small group	Scheduled on site or at an agreed location	Attendees only	Semi-private	Temporal; recorded in varying detail; may warrant press coverage	Somewhat public recognition; Improved personal relationships
Large-multiple donor event	Schedule on site or at an agreed location	Attendees only, unless covered by press or otherwise publicized	Public	Temporal; recorded in varying detail; may warrant press coverage	Public recognition; Improved personal relationships
Donor gifts	Items given to donor for personal use/enjoyment	Donor, anyone with whom the donor shares it and the donor record	Private	At the donors discretion	Limited to the value placed on sharing the items with others
A book, framed photograph or piece of artwork	Items given to donor for personal use/enjoyment	Donor, anyone with whom the donor shares it and the donor record	Private	At the donor's discretion	Limited to the value placed on sharing the item with others

Activity	Method	Audience	Destination	Permanence	Legacy Building Potential
Plaques or awards	Items given to donor for personal or public use/ enjoyment	Donor, anyone with whom the donor shares it and the donor record	Limited public	At the donor's discretion	Limited to the value placed on sharing the item with others
T-shirts, hats and other promotional items	Items given to donor for personal or public use/ enjoyment	Donor, anyone with whom the donor shares it and the donor record	Limited public	At the donor's discretion	Provides opportunity for the donor to endorse the organization by using the item in public
Donor testimonials in print, on-line or included in a display	Print or digital	General public	Public	Varies	Increases general awareness and understanding of the donor
Donor list in print or on website	Print or digital	General public	Public	Varies	Increases general awareness of the donor
Donor lists in public displays	Print or digital	General public	Public	Varies	Increases general awareness of the donor
Plaques for individual donors	Permanent graphics or product solutions	General public	Public	Usually considered permanent	Increases general awareness and understanding of the donor

Structure every donor recognition activity so that it provides benefits to the organization as well as to the donor. Obviously, it would be wrong to take advantage of the donor or violate a request for anonymity. Maximizing every investment, however, is an obligation of good stewardship. It can be done tastefully and with no compromise to the donor experience.

These are examples of multipurpose recognition planning:

1. When a donor is meeting with a key leader at the organization, highlights from the conversation can be documented as a blog post, complete with photography and quotes from the donor and the organization's representative.

2. When a student writes an especially good letter of thanks to the sponsor of his or her scholarship, some of the language may be repurposed as a pull quote in the next scholarship solicitation.

3. A branded tag can be included with any premium or promotional item to provide donors with the most up-to-date talking points about the organization.

Gifts, premiums, swag, tchotchke–no matter what you call them, these relatively small items given to a donor as a takeaway are still common. They serve two purposes: they are a token of appreciation and they (theoretically) give the donor cause to talk about the organization with others. They must be carefully crafted, therefore, to do both of these things effectively. Done well, they're fun. Done poorly, they can be embarrassing. Whether fun or embarrassing, they lack any real recognition value and, given my professional druthers, would be moved from donor recognition to the marketing category. The fact that these items are a standing component in your organization's recognition arsenal cannot substitute for a more meaningful and effective form of donor recognition, even at the smallest gift levels.

Annual publications, generically known as honor rolls, were once the norm but are losing popularity. They are expensive to produce and do not sway a donor's affinity for the organization. The dollars spent preparing and disseminating a list of this sort might be better invested in other donor recognition practices. Let us not throw out the baby with the bathwater, however. The ability to maintain and accurately report donor names for the purpose of donor recognition remains important. Maintaining a separate field in the donor record for "formal donor name" is a wise practice that benefits everything from sending invitations to maintaining donor lists within a display.

Thank you events are undergoing scrutiny. Most donor relations professionals find that large scale events are becoming more expensive to produce and aren't resulting in greater attendance or donor satisfaction. Be clear about the goals for each event and compare each component and expense to its contribution to the goal. Event strategy must be based on the desired outcome, not the habits formed by past years' events or the talents of a new event planner.

Facility-based donor recognition, such as donor walls and plaques, are a luxury for some organizations but are a staple practice, especially as a component in major giving programs. Campaign listings, leadership giving, cumulative giving and planned giving displays are now seen as frequently as the more longstanding annual giving donor walls. Organizations benefit from different listing types, largely depending on the audience that will see the display. Some organizations have moved to digital displays for ease of updating. For a brief while, donor lists were transitioning to websites, but that is becoming less frequent as it has been found that the sites are rarely visited by donors or prospects. Furthermore, many organizations are concerned about issues of donor privacy and making the donor list too easily available to prospect researchers.

Maximizing the Investment in Permanent Public Donor Recognition

Plaques and displays—those elements most likely to take a permanent public place in an organization's facilities—are my area of expertise. Twenty years in the field gives me insight to make a bold assertion: campus-based donor recognition should be an investment in talking about donors to the general audience, not simply a method for generating a positive response from the individual donor. The donor will likely see the plaque or display once or twice. The people who work, study or are served in the building will see it every day. With that in mind, what does the location, quality and content of the donor recognition product say to the general audience about your organization and its attitudes about philanthropy?

Donor recognition on campus is inherently public and usually permanent. It is an investment that warrants careful coordination with the architecture surrounding it, the organization's messaging standards and the routine practices of those who will be responsible for maintaining it. Donor recognition in a facility must communicate the organization's attitude toward philanthropy without one needing to read a single word. It must be distinctive in material and location and branded to the character of the organization. Being conscious of issues of style and design includes choosing materials that are durable and timeless. Finding a prominent location and good lighting is as important as attending meticulously to word choice, grammar, typography and punctuation. Moderating the prominence of the organization's logo helps keep focus on the donors listed. These subtle details communicate volumes about the organization's appreciation of its contributing philanthropists.

Above all, written copy must be compelling and convey more than the donor's name. Who is this person; why did he or she care about this organization; when was the gift made; and what effect was it meant to have? The process of developing that story—diving deep with the donor and making the story as specific to the relationship with this organization as possible—is a great stewardship opportunity. The reasons why the donor made the gift can be lost over time when recognition is generic. For the recognition to be meaningful to a broad audience and provide true legacy-building, it must include enough detail to differentiate one donor from the next by more than just the name. Each piece must include a minimal statement of who the donor is and why he or she decided to make this gift. This extra effort adds meaning for the donor and value for the general audience. Universally, better storytelling leads to better donor recognition and stronger donor relationships. When the organization demonstrates its ability to tell a donor's story and connect it to details of accomplishing its own mission, true recognition is achieved.

Lettering to identify a space, even if the message includes the donor name, is not recognition. This type of lettering originated as a wayfinding device known as a destination graphic. If a gift is significant enough to warrant a space-naming opportunity, the donor relationship is important enough to warrant a little storytelling. Developing an element that provides the opportunity to tell that story may inspire other prospective donors. In most cases, the story is presented on a plaque in or near the physical space, but new technologies have expanded the ways to share this meaningful information. There are great examples of virtual tours or print collateral used to enhance donor recognition and improve the user experience.

Today, there are many different ways to achieve the variety of donor recognition outcomes required to effectively reflect the variety of gifts received by an organization. This chart illustrates some of the most frequent types of facility-based donor recognition and the appropriate methods for each display type.

Figure 2: Facility-based Donor Recognition product format

		Relationship	Cautions	Recognition Product Norms	Typical Recognition Format
Not Well-suited to Electronic Media	Campaign Listing	• Time-limited • Volume known • Immediate focus	• Often the fundraiser's focus	• Usually presented as a list with categories • Appropriate to artistic interpretation	• Ranges from on-line list to printed keepsake book to permanent display
	Facility Based Naming Opportunities	• Single moment in history • Volume known • Immediate focus	• Often the architect's focus	• Usually a family of sign sizes based on gift amount • Often includes dimensional letters • Open to location/donor specific inter-pretation	• Individual plaques at the location or grouped in a public area
Easily Presented via Electronic Media	Endowment Giving	• Often on going, multi-gen-erational relation-ship • Value of the naming opportu-nity grows over time		• Often ad-dressed via events and reporting, no public signage	• On-line or print lists • Occasionally honored with displays at the highest levels
	Special Projects	• Often time-limited • Smaller, insular groups of donors (knowl-edge or passion specific)	• Often managed by an individual, not the institution	• Large format print graphics • Usually presented as a list with categories • Affordable update method	• Varies, depending on project type, budget and communication strategy

		Relationship	Cautions	Recognition Product Norms	Typical Recognition Format
Easily Presented via Electronic Media	**Annual Giving**	• Time-limited • Volume known • Immediate focus	• Should clearly indicate that one can "give now" to be on the next list	• Large format print graphics • Usually presented as a list with categories • Easy-to-manage update method	• On-line or print lists in easily updated displays • Lends well to electronic media
	Cumulative Giving	• List with irregular growth patterns • Requires flexibility for donors to "move up" the list	• Imply permanence • Communicate "elite nature" of the list	• Usually presented as a list with categories	• Permanent components displayed in a prominent location
	Planned Giving	• List, often without categories	• List criteria vary • Avoid expense of adding a marker for deceased donors	• Permanent display once volume is sufficient	• Permanent components displayed in a prominent location
	Volunteer Leadership	• Flexible volume and format to manage changes in service structure	• List criteria vary	• Large format print graphics, with or without permanent plaques	• On-line or print lists in easily updated displays • Lends well to electronic media

Identifying and Using Efficient Program Management Tools

Many organizations would benefit from standardization to make recognition practices efficient and more effective.[3] Consistency, coordinated branding, cost-effective implementation and maintenance procedures must be carefully planned. Other teams—internal and external—should be engaged. A balance should be struck so that objectives, roles, budgets and schedules are clearly communicated without sacrificing creativity and spontaneity.

Donor recognition standards and guidelines are now seen more frequently; sometimes the information is codified under the title of policy. Upon close study, however, many are really nothing more than mandated formulas for establishing naming opportunities or a list of recognition societies.[4] Comprehensive donor recognition program documentation must address all types of donor recognition and include design guidelines and information for administering the program.

For practical reasons, the documentation may be negotiated with other departments, such as the communications, marketing and facilities teams. The documents often undergo review and formal approval by a top-level administrator or board. The final product is, however, a living document requiring occasional additions and adjustments. To that end, it is typically maintained by one staff person or a small group and may be scheduled for routine review and revision.

Donor recognition documentation should detail the following:

1. Type and amount of giving

2. Content and product design guidelines

3. Clearly stated roles and responsibilities for executing the program

4. Specific schedule and budget expectations

The most comprehensive documents address a host of activities including announcements, event, mementos, lists as well as plaques and displays. The following chart outlines the recommended contents for the documentation of a comprehensive donor recognition program. Emphasis can be placed on different components depending on the type and size of the organization and its fundraising programs. For instance, a hospital might have greater focus on annual and employee giving campaigns while an academic institution might have more instances of naming opportunities for virtual opportunities, such as scholarships, faculty positions and programs. A smaller institution might merge several lists into a single display while a larger one might have multiple outlets for the same information.

Figure 3: Typical contents of donor recognition standards and guidelines documentation

Section	Detail

Statement of Purpose	1. Mission, Vision and Values statements for the organization
	2. Mission, Vision and Values statements for donor relations and stewardship
	3. Guiding principles of donor relations and stewardship
	4. Statement of the purpose and scope of the donor recognition standards and guidelines
	5. Definitions
	6. Reference to related policies and procedures including:
	   a. Regulation or governance affecting the standards and guidelines
	   b. Naming opportunity gift minimums and value calculation models
	   c. Cancellation of naming rights
	   d. Timing for donor recognition practices
	   e. Gift agreement template and regulations
	   f. Pledge policies
	   g. Style guidelines
	7. List of stakeholders by role and responsibility, with contact information
	8. Implementation procedures

Donor Recognition	1. Giving programs by gift category
	   a. Major gifts resulting in naming opportunities
	   b. Major gift contributions to existing funds
	   c. Planned giving
	   d. Annual giving, with any subcategories
	      i. Individual giving
	      ii. Corporate and foundation giving
	      iii. Faculty, staff, physician or employee giving
	      iv. Student or parent giving
	      v. Grateful patient or beneficiary giving
	2. Stewardship activities matrix (what is done, when and by whom)
	3. Recognition opportunity location plans (volume may require a separate document)
	4. Inventory of named and available opportunities
	5. Hardscape products overview

Section	Detail
Gift Announcement Protocol	1. Media announcement guidelines 2. Social media announcement guidelines 3. Website announcement guidelines 4. Stationery templates 5. Print collateral templates

Donor Recognition Products Overview	1. Naming Opportunities Recognition Overview
	   a. Interior Area Naming Sign Components Hierarchy
	   b. Exterior Area Naming Sign Components Hierarchy
	   c. Grouped Naming Sign Components Hierarchy
	   d. Destination Graphic Overview
	   e. Building Naming Overview
	   f. Campus Naming Overview
	   g. Virtual Naming Recognition Overview
	2. Centralized Philanthropy Listings
	   a. Cumulative Giving
	   b. Planned Giving
	   c. Endowments
	   d. Tributes and Memorial Gifts
	   e. Volunteer Recognition
	   f. Service and Leadership Recognition
	3. Electronic Media Content Guidelines
	4. Storytelling Venues (Donor testimonials, history exhibits, success stories)

Design Guidelines	1. Fabrication documentation including
	   a. Sizes
	   b. Materials, finishes and colors
	   c. Construction methods
	   d. Layout templates
	   e. Typical installation guidelines

Implementation Procedures	1. Program support, implementation and maintenance roles and responsibilities 2. Workflow diagram 3. Product ordering information, including order forms and known pricing 4. Assets and access to donor information 5. Record-keeping directives 6. Review and approval process 7. Budget and schedule forecast
Pending Additions	1. Notes and reference to outstanding issues, new circumstances and known improvements to the documentation
Examples	1. Dated record of examples including vendor approvals and photographs of completed projects
References	1. Audit of pre-existing donor recognition, with explanation as available 2. Review of peer institution examples 3. Peer institution surveys or interviews

The documentation must include design directives and a specific review and approval process. Design documentation can take one of two forms or some combination of the two:

1. Standards: a set of rules resulting in a similar look within tightly monitored variations

2. Guidelines: instructions that inform the process by which the design develops, often resulting in a variety of different outcomes that follow a similar design logic

The best recognition positively reflects the character of the organization and tells a story that is specific, timeless and meaningful to all audiences. To realize these qualities, the organization must identify and hone a specific voice. That exercise typically coincides with efforts within the marketing and communications team and may be referred to as the editorial voice.

In terms of donor recognition, representing the character of the organization involves developing a style guide that outlines a consistent approach to design that results in a system of similar products with a uniform, or at least planned, level of quality and tone.

Content development guidelines will dictate how to refer to the organization, its units, departments, facilities, services, other activities and accomplishments. There should be consistency in how the donor is referenced, although the details must take into consideration donor preference. Negotiation may be required and standards may only be accomplished over time. Specific directives about the use of the organization's logo or seal and the approved coincidence of a donor mark or logo are also addressed.

Every donor recognition program must address material considerations as well. Material choices must be durable. Assume that recognition product will be in place for several years at least. Plaque and display products should be constructed of readily available materials. The best designs do not depend on a single source to perpetuate the program.

Most important, the program must include enough options to remain versatile if new circumstances arise. For instance, institutions often underestimate the volume of growth in their giving programs and do not sufficiently plan for future expansion. When considering new technologies, it is wise to a create budget for routine maintenance and hardware and software upgrades. Large format print graphics have made annual list updates far easier, yet the materials and processes involved in this type of printing change rapidly. Technological change is an even more influential factor when planning the long-term viability of an electronic display.

Analyzing Return On Investment for Donor Recognition

Volume of activity and subjective feedback are all that can be measured when donor recognition activities lack strategic objectives. This type of monitoring is a worthy starting place; however, as a program matures, monitoring donor retention, increased giving and enhanced engagement must be worked into the plan. Systematic measurement of success requires a set of predetermined goals and gathering information appropriate for analysis.

Using an iterative approach to execute, review and revise donor recognition plans demands recording goals per project or as a part of an annual work plan. Detailed progress notes should track both successes and failures. Information recorded should include dates, suppliers, costs, schedules and procedures, as well as photographs documenting events and product outcomes. This data should be integrated into donor records with reporting protocols. The next person managing donor recognition will appreciate this level of documentation.

I typically recommend monitoring three factors to gauge the effectiveness of improved donor recognition practices:

> *Donor satisfaction*: In some situations, my firm is engaged because there is a need to satisfy one donor or a specific group of donors. In that case, anecdotal feedback is the best measure

of success. More often, we are asked to address the recognition of one or more groups of donors. In those situations, we ask for baseline measurement of donor giving history in order to study any increases in gift amount or giving frequency. We also look for improvements in donor retention and engagement, such as better event attendance or increased volunteerism. For each of these measures we accept that there is a complex set of factors influencing changes in donor behavior, but we maintain accurate records of changes following new donor recognition activity.

Efficiency: Prior to implementing a new donor recognition practice or improving a procedure, we survey staff to clarify the current situation and identify known problems. Once the new practice is in place, we recommend repeat surveys, usually annually, to verify that perceptions have improved and compare those perceptions to more objective data like time to completion for selected tasks and specific reduction in costs.

Internal awareness: One of the overlooked benefits of donor recognition program improvement is increased awareness of philanthropy across the organization, often referred to as an improved "culture of philanthropy." Again, with the client's permission, we survey or conduct limited interviews across the organization to establish a baseline for organization-wide understanding of the role of the fundraising team and/or philanthropy to the accomplishment of mission. Immediately following rollout of the donor recognition program and then at one-year intervals we repeat the survey or interview and monitor the results. Our findings support the claim that more public donor recognition, especially that which includes storytelling about the donors, improves awareness of and affinity for the philanthropic supporters of the organization.

Planning for Change in the Donor Recognition Program

With twenty years in this field, I've gained perspective about the flexibility required of a comprehensive donor recognition program.

Strategy isn't static and a successful donor recognition program will have to change over time.

There are a limited number of factors that cause donor recognition program changes:

1. Shift in organizational or fundraising strategy, often as a result of leadership transition

2. Increased longevity/complexity in the organization's donor relationships (the better you do your job, the more challenging it becomes)

3. Increases in the number of donor relationships to be managed (again, the better you do your job, the more challenging it becomes)

4. Technology and material advances

Here are a few of the most important principles for managing the evolution of a long-standing donor recognition program:

1. Check all pending decisions against current strategy; don't introduce new tactics that aren't aligned with strategy.

2. Realign donor recognition strategy with organizational strategy as needed; annual review is warranted, at a minimum.

3. Proactively manage buy-in from leadership and other stakeholders in the program; reacquaint others with the program structure on a frequent basis by keeping them abreast of projects completed and pending changes in the documentation.

4. Make sure the program is broad and integrated enough to withstand leadership change or the loss of a key employee or vendor relationship.

5. Compare the practices of different units or departments and seek consistency.

6. Donors tend to view their giving from a cumulative, organization-wide perspective. Be careful about segmenting donor recognition to align with internal record-keeping. Always show awareness of the full relationship with the donor.

7. Be careful about setting precedents; the "biggest ever" donor of today will soon have peers.

8. Consider whether a given activity can be repeated for any other donor meeting the same criteria.

9. Prepare to manage exceptions: they can come from donor demands or limits resulting from new architecture, budget or time constraints.

10. Assume the program documentation will be largely revamped at least once a decade.

11. Plan for increased naming opportunity gift minimums over time.

12. Prepare for emerging technology.

13. Anticipate longer-lasting, more complex relationships with donors that will require new creative solutions for recognition.

14. Assume that the volume of donors will grow over time. Forecast often to best manage time and dollar investments.

15. Expect shifts in perspective as evidence that you are doing your job right and learning from your experience.

16. Encourage the donor recognition program to grow and evolve with the organization.

Conclusion

A comprehensive and strategic donor recognition program is a critical indicator of an organization's ability to build strong relationships with its donors and increase philanthropic support of its mission. Success is achieved through alignment of the day-to-day donor recognition practices with organizational goals and priorities. Program documentation should address all types of donor recognition activities and product outcomes. The program is not a rigid set of rules, but rather a flexible tool for managing the organization's efforts to communicate with and about its donors. The donor recognition program is used to reward and engage additional philanthropy from current and prospective donors and to build a broad and reliable culture of philanthropy.

Creating a strategy for donor recognition starts with understanding that recognition is about saying thank you in ways that celebrate the donors while highlighting the unique character of the organization. All donor recognition is a balance between the needs, goals and resources of the organization and the effort to thank and further engage the donor. When done well, donor recognition includes sufficient storytelling to make the donor known to an ever-evolving audience.

Strategy helps avoid errors and omissions in donor recognition outcomes. Recognition is elevated above a random assortment of activities or an imitation of what other organizations are doing when it delivers a message that honors the individuality of the donor and his or her role in accomplishing the organization's mission. Donor recognition moves from being an obligation to be checked off a list to a donor-centric, organization-specific celebration of philanthropy.

Anne Manner-McLarty is the managing editor of the *Journal of Donor Relations and Stewardship*. She founded Heurista in 2011, a leading resource for consulting specific to donor relations and stewardship, with particular expertise in the donor recognition program design and implementation. She is a long-standing member of the Association of Donor Relations Professionals and served on the ADRP board 2012-2014.

Endnotes

[1] Barry, Frank, Lawrence Henze, David Lamb, and Katherine Swank. Cultivating Lifelong Donors: Stewardship and the Fundraising Pyramid. PDF. Blackbaud, Inc., 2010. Pg.39.

[2] Donor Relations and Stewardship Defined. PDF. Association of Donor Relations Professionals. Accessed January 25, 2016.

[3] New Oxford American Dictionary (3rd ed.).

[4] Cinconte, Barbara L., CFRE. Developing Fundraising Policies and Procedures: Best Practices for Transparency. PDF. Arlington, Va.: Association of Fundraising Professionals, 2007. Pg. 23-26.

References/Bibliography

Best Practices in Donor Recognition, Association of Donor Relations Professionals. Accessed January 25, 2016.

http://www.adrp.net/assets/documents/bestpractices/adrp_best_practices-donor_recognition.pdf.

Barry, Frank, Lawrence Henze, David Lamb, and Katherine Swank. Cultivating Lifelong Donors: Stewardship and the Fundraising Pyramid. PDF. Blackbaud, Inc., 2010. https://www.blackbaud.com/files/resources/downloads/Book_CultivatingLifelongDonors.pdf.

Best Practice in Policy & Procedure Manual Creation. PDF. Association of Donor Relations Professionals, May 2012. http://www.adrp.net/assets/documents/adrp_bp_policy_manual_05.2012.pdf.

Ciconte, Barbara L., CFRE. Developing Fundraising Policies and Procedures: Best Practices for Accountability and Transparency. PDF. Arlington, VA: Association of Fundraising Professionals, 2007.

Fundraising Fundamentals, Section 10.7, Gift Recognition Policies. Council for Advancement and Support of Education. https://www.case.org/Publications_and_Products/Fundraising_Fundamentals_Intro/Fundraising_Fundamentals_section_10/Fundraising_Fundamentals_section_107.html.

Gifford, Gayle. "Essential Elements Of A Donor Recognition Program - CharityChannel Press." CharityChannel Press. September 10, 2002. Accessed March 15, 2016. http://charitychannel.com/essential-elements-of-a-donor-recognition-program/.

Grace, Kay Sprinkel. *Beyond Fundraising: New Strategies for Nonprofit Innovation and Investment.* 2nd Edition ed. Hoboken, N.J.: John Wiley & Sons, 2005.
Rewire Your Thinking about Donor Recognition Policy! PDF. Robin E. William Incorporated, 2009.
http://www.rewinc.com/wp-content/uploads/2012/11/DR-Policy.pdf.

Rogers, Kate. "Donor Recognition Is More Than A Trinket - The NonProfit Times." *The NonProfit Times.* May 15, 2010. Accessed April 11, 2016. http://www.thenonprofittimes.com/news-articles/donor-recognition-is-more-than-a-trinket/.

Roth, Kimberlee. "Smaller Charities Need Creativity and Care When Recognizing Donors." *The Chronicle of Philanthropy.* March 20, 2003. Accessed April 11, 2016. https://philanthropy.com/article/Smaller-Charities-Need/183745.

Sagrestano, Brian M., and Robert E. Wahlers. *The Philanthropic Planning Companion: A Charitable Giving Guide for Fundraising.* Hoboken, N.J. : John Wiley & Sons, 2012.

United States. National Park Service. "Donor Recognition Plans." National Parks Service. Accessed April 11, 2016. https://www.nps.gov/partnerships/donor_partner_plan.htm.

Book 1 | June 2016

Required or Elective? The Importance of Creative Writing Skill
to the Practice of Donor Relations and Stewardship

Required or Elective? The Importance of Creative Writing Skill to the Practice of Donor Relations and Stewardship

By Daphne B. Powell

In this article, the author argues for the importance of writing as a fundamental skill in donor relations and stewardship. Definitions of types of writing are presented along with how they might be useful in donor relations and stewardship. Hiring good writers is reviewed, with attention to testing skills during an interview. Developing and enhancing writing skills through training and practice are discussed. Organizational structure and distribution of writing assignments are also reviewed. A list of books and other resources conclude the discussion.

Content:

- Writing as an essential skill in donor relations and stewardship
- Types of writing
- Writing style and writing for someone else
- Staff roles and writing skills
- Developing skill as a writer
- Style guides and writing conformity
- References for further information

Glossary:

- Expository Writing: The main purpose of expository writing is to explain a concept or idea while including details for support. Support is provided through facts, not opinions. It is mostly used in textbook writing, how-to articles, recipes, news stories, and business, technical, or scientific writing.

- Persuasive Writing: Like expository writing, persuasive writing uses specific details and examples for support, but opinion is largely used with emotion playing a large role in affecting the reader. It is mostly used in opinion/editorial pieces, advertisements, reviews (books, music, movies, restaurants, etc.), letters of recommendation or complaint, and cover letters.

- Descriptive Writing: The main purpose of descriptive writing is to entertain versus inform and is found in fiction and poetry. It is most often used in journal writing, nature writing, and descriptive passages in fiction.

Book 1 | June 2016

Required or Elective? The Importance of Creative Writing Skill
to the Practice of Donor Relations and Stewardship

- Narrative Writing: Like descriptive writing, narrative writing entertains, but by telling a story rather than through the beauty of it's verse. It is most often used in novels, short stories, novellas, poetry, autobiographies and biographies, anecdotes, and oral histories.

Author's note: I want to begin by stating that I don't consider myself an excellent writer. I had wonderful teachers throughout my youth who taught grammar and punctuation well. I was one of those kids who enjoyed diagramming sentences and singing along with the Saturday morning Schoolhouse Rock episodes. I managed to pass my audition for creative writing at the Alabama School of Fine Arts, but there were many students with greater talent for writing poetry and fiction. I do feel, however, that I have an innate skill that has been nurtured and developed—one that is significantly lacking in the professional world today, and that skill helps me in making good decisions for UAB as I oversee a portion of what the university is communicating to donors. In this article, I will talk about that skill—one of recognizing good writing and having a sense for what makes a good story. We need this in our practice to bring our donors along in their philanthropy to our institutions.

Introduction

At UAB, I am responsible for gift agreements for named endowments, spaces, and programs; for ensuring that governing rules are met; for setting the standards for donor recognition university-wide; and for managing the recognition of and reporting to our major donors who have made gifts of $25,000 and above. Recognition components include acknowledgment by university leadership, along with the preparation of documents for our board of trustees, and management of and consultation on physical donor recognition projects. Reporting includes endowment reports and impact reports that are prepared for all major gift donors to the university. Our office does not handle donor cultivation and recognition events or the aspects of donor communications which for UAB includes donor newsletters, on-demand print publications and proposals, web communications, and social media.

A writer is a person who uses written words in various styles and techniques to communicate ideas. Is being a writer a requirement for being the conductor of donor relations and stewardship activities at your institution? Arguments can be made for and against this notion, but my personal opinion is that it is essential for the leader of these efforts to be at least a semi-skilled writer, among the many other talents necessary to carry out the mission of the department. It is also critical that this individual has an understanding and appreciation for what creative writing means to the practice of donor relations and stewardship.

This article will take you through my thinking about why creative writing is important, the general types of writing styles, what aspects of a donor relations and stewardship program are defined by good writing, what types of writing are needed to enhance the donor relations and stewardship programs, what organizational structure dictates concerning the disposition of writers within an institution, how to manage writers, and what resources I would personally recommend to develop and enhance writing skills.

Job Responsibilities

There are various forms of donor relations and stewardship departments. Some are largely focused on duties such as acknowledgments and reporting, while others have a broad array of responsibilities that include not only all aspects of donor reporting and recognition, but also the management of scholarship awards to students. There are those that pile even more under this umbrella, including prospect research, proposal writing, and donor communications, along with social media.

Acknowledgment writing is one of the key elements of any donor relations and stewardship department. If these letters are the only communication with donors that your shop handles, it is critical that creative writing play a part in what you do. Penelope Burk has revealed through donor surveys that brief but meaningful correspondence in a timely fashion is key to donor retention and to increased giving. The same letter to all donors just doesn't carry as much weight as a personal letter to each donor which reflects gratitude and impact and leaves the person feeling good about the gift made.

Types of Writing Skill Needed

Any professional must have a general foundation in writing, grammar, punctuation, and proofreading, but particularly those in a relationship-based career. For some activities associated with the donor relations and stewardship profession, a solid foundation is preferred. As long as an understanding of how to communicate well is there, an individual is likely to learn and grow in time through mentorship, education, and networking opportunities.

There are four main types of writing styles (compiled from online sources):

1. Expository Writing:
    The main purpose of expository writing is to explain a concept or idea while including details for support. Support is provided through facts, not opinions. It is mostly used in textbook writing, how-to articles, recipes, news stories, and business, technical, or scientific writing.
    -   Expository writing usually explains something in a process.
    -   Expository writing is often equipped with facts and figures.
    -   Expository writing is usually in a logical order and sequence.

2. Persuasive Writing:
    Like expository writing, specific details and examples are used for support in persuasive writing, but opinion is largely used with emotion playing a large role in affecting the reader. It is mostly used in opinion/editorial pieces, advertisements, reviews (books, music, movies, restaurants, etc.), letters of recommendation or complaint, and cover letters.
    -   Persuasive writing is equipped with reasons, arguments, and justifications.
    -   In persuasive writing, the author takes a stand and asks you to agree with his or her point of view.
    -   It often asks for readers to do something about the situation (the call-to-action).

3. Descriptive Writing:
   The main purpose of descriptive writing is to entertain versus inform and is found in fiction and poetry. It is most often used in journal writing, nature writing, and descriptive passages in fiction.
   - Descriptive writing is often poetic in nature
   - Descriptive writing describes places, people, events, situations, or locations in a highly detailed manner.
   - The author communicates what the reader will see, hear, taste, smell or feel

4. Narrative Writing:
   Like descriptive writing, narrative writing is for entertaining the reader but through the telling of a story versus through the beauty of its verse. It is most often used in novels, short stories, novellas, poetry, autobiographies and biographies, anecdotes, and oral histories.
   - In narrative writing, a person tells a story or event.
   - Narrative writing has characters and dialogue.
   - Narrative writing has definite and logical beginnings, intervals, and endings.
   - Narrative writing often has situations like actions, motivational events, and disputes or conflicts with their eventual solutions.

For our donor relations and stewardship efforts, we primarily use expository and persuasive writing to state the facts and strengthen the case for ongoing support from the donor. When I am looking for a writer, therefore, I am looking for someone who can write well while explaining a process or a measurable result of a gift and who can complete a sufficient amount of research to logically and persuasively write about a giving impact area.

I also look for the ability of that person to write like someone else. I will go into greater detail later in the article about the tests that I use to help screen applicants for a writing position, but when I ask candidates to complete the letter-writing component of this test, I give background on our leader and ask the individual to write the letter as close to what she or he thinks that person would say. The candidate not knowing the individual makes this test somewhat unreliable, but it is still an indicator of how well the candidate can "hear voices."

Hearing someone's voice and translating it into words on paper is not always an easy task. To be frank, I firmly believe that voices tend to be regional and that more often than not it takes an exceptional—not just above average, but exceptional—writer to "get" a voice that is outside what he or she is accustomed to. When you have people who believe they are strong writers and know everything about the process of writing for another when they really don't, the effort of "righting" that person to your path can be futile because of this lack of awareness. Perhaps there is even internal resistance to change or doing things in a different way.

Is there any hope for the strong writer who cannot hear a voice outside his or her own head? I believe that there are three approaches to solving this problem. First of all, the ability of a writer to track the voice of another person when writing a letter or preparing remarks can be tested during an interview. You can present a candidate for a writing position with documents from people within the organization for whom the candidate might be preparing documents. Can the candidate point out in the documents the elements that constitute the voice of the other person? Can the candidate emulate the voice of the other person in a writing exercise conducted during the interview? This would most often be composing a letter of acknowledgment for a leader of the organization.

Second, if measuring the sensitivity of a new writer to the voice of other people for whom the writer may be responsible for letters or remarks hasn't been completely successful, providing training during the early months of the writer's employment may bring the writer into greater conformity with the other person's voice. This process may take a considerable amount of time, but the positive result that may ensue will have considerable value for the organization. Good writers are hard to find.

Finally, if the assessment process during hiring and training in early employment do not help to develop the new writer into an emulator of the executive's voice, there may be opportunities to assign a good writer to other projects. It might be that the writer is better at exposition than creativity, or has skill at persuasion. These are writing styles that the organization may need and finding a place for a good writer and seeking the "other voice" talent may be a reasonable course of action.

What's Culture Got to Do With It?

We all know the communication of ideas is important to the profession, but that may not necessarily mean that the director of an institution's stewardship program must be a talented writer. In many respects, it will depend on the organization itself, along with its particular donor base, marketing strategy, structure, and culture. These unique features define how stewardship fits into the fundraising paradigm at each organization, and when certain aspects of donor relations and stewardship are handled by other related departments, it can completely alter the dynamics of the skillset needed to direct the defined aspects of that organization's donor relations and stewardship efforts.

There are a multitude of consultants and firms who have proven through studies and surveys that written communication can make or break the monetary fundraising goal and related efforts to recruit and retain donors. These studies confirm what those who have spent time in the field know inherently. In my 17 years in the fundraising world— from starting regular stewardship reporting to donors, to leading fundraising initiatives for various campus units, to developing an ever-evolving donor relations program—it is clear that having a way with words, both written and spoken, boosts success.

The skillset needed for directing the unit's responsibilities greatly depends on how your organization is structured, how donor relations and stewardship are defined, and what is squeezing under your umbrella that doesn't really fit. Several organizational scenarios follow, and each might require a different level of creative writing skill for the person overseeing donor relations and stewardship.

As discussed above, just because someone is hired for the wrong job doesn't mean that he or she isn't a strong candidate for another position on the team. More and more managers restructure their units to accommodate the strengths, as well as the weaknesses, of all team members. When I was faced with a situation such as this, we offered the incumbent opportunities that better fit her skills within other areas of development. We recognized this writer's strengths and built upon them to our mutual satisfaction.

The Lone Ranger

I started out in the new position of stewardship coordinator within the donor services team at UAB. There was no designated office of stewardship; donor relations was not a phrase widely used at the time; and my major responsibility was to implement endowment reporting at UAB. Soon I realized what a demanding job it would be to coordinate the information needed, write the reports, and ensure the appropriate people were receiving the letters. I also saw the need for an organized structure and approach to all aspects of donor recognition and stewardship at the university. Despite limited resources and a tendency to be given "special project" assignments, I became The Lone Ranger for Stewardship, working toward a goal of structured donor recognition versus being just a simple reporting arm of gift processing.

Over the years, I can't tell you how many times I have heard from donor relations and stewardship professionals who are the only individuals in their organizations responsible for donor recognition. This doesn't even begin to touch on those organizations that are so small and with such limited budgets that one person is prospecting, proposal writing, soliciting, acknowledging, recognizing, and reporting on gifts. Whew!

I do have some advice for those in this business who are working alone to appreciate those who have been generous to the organization and to reach out to those who might see the organization as a worthy investment. Since this article is about the importance of writing to the practice of donor relations and stewardship and to realizing our goal of keeping our supporters close, I will say that selecting a few opportunities to write a well-crafted letter or speak publicly about the effect of philanthropy on the realization of the mission of the organization are more important than organizing an event or preparing multiple endowment reports. What good writing does is position us to select the opportunities to say something important to a few critical philanthropists and to the larger group of those who are developing their philanthropy to our organization. Use your resources to speak with gratitude to the individuals who make a difference now and to speak about the mission to a larger group who are beginning to pay attention.

Regardless of the litany of duties that could be thrust upon an individual, the lone ranger must have a versatile writing style, adapting to the specific assignment, audience, and messenger. Being rich in words and able to express them both orally and in writing are critical skills for the donor relations writer. There is no doubt that being an effective communicator in this role is essential for success. How does someone become rich in words? Clearly, word richness means possessing and deploying a significant vocabulary. Building a vocabulary comes from being a reader as well as a writer. There are many sources available in print and on the Internet for enriching one's vocabulary. A few examples are listed at the end of this article. Opportunities to enrich a writer's vocabulary exist within the organization as well. Writers should attend as many programs offered by the organization as possible to build a rich organizational vocabulary as well.

Centralized versus Decentralized

Many institutions, frequently in higher education but also in organizations with multiple campuses or a national presence, have a central office that handles gift processing and major gift development, while they have fundraisers assigned to various units or regions of the organization. The larger the organization the more that the job responsibilities will be more focused within a central office. Our team operates in a decentralized environment where we have specific individuals assigned to focused responsibilities based on their performance strengths.

Having a centralized donor relations and stewardship office gives us the opportunity to speak to our donors in one voice. In large organizations, a few donors may support a number of units, and the central donor relations office can deliver institutional messages to these donors in a seamless and standardized manner. The program units themselves can focus on managing the relationship with these donors rather than segmenting their efforts into fundraising and stewardship.

This does not mean that the units don't have donor relations and stewardship responsibilities. In a centralized effort, production-based donor relations and stewardship, such as acknowledgment writing and report generation, and the activities I manage at UAB, are efficiently managed so that gift officers can cultivate prospects and solicit new gifts. Our chairs are warm so that gift officers' chairs can be cold.

Delivering a consistent message in a centralized donor relations and stewardship organization requires as much coordination and cooperation as operating in a decentralized organization. Understanding the emerging relationships with the donors comes from collaboration with the units, but coordination with a communications office and the executive staff in a centralized environment means greater efficiency of operation.

Executive leadership must create and maintain an effective centralized donor relations and stewardship effort because only the executive can overcome a feeling in the organization that donors belong to one unit or another. Controlling the resources for donor relations and stewardship is one way to press the issue of centralized services. Surveying donors and auditing the donor relations and stewardship work of the units can help to press the cause of centralized activities.

Staffing and Work Distribution

In my department at UAB, I have a *reporting specialist*, a *communications specialist*, and a *stewardship associate*. These three individuals have different, complementary skills. The reporting specialist must be able to produce narrative-based writing to communicate the messages provided by students, faculty, and staff of the university. The communications specialist focuses on descriptive and persuasive writing, and also adapts messages for different constituents from a variety of university leaders. The stewardship associate focuses on assuring quality and managing production and works closely with me to understand these components as we review various materials for distribution to a multitude of individuals and organizations.

Stewardship reports are a good example of how work flows through my department. Reports are initiated by the reporting specialist, who passes along a full creative report to the stewardship associate. After the stewardship associate proofreads the report, he sends it to the senior director for comments. The report is then returned to the reporting specialist for corrections and to the stewardship associate for production and distribution. From the beginning to the distribution takes about two days. This is a constant process, and the work is tracked using a software system call WorkFront. This system is not perfect, but it does keep us on track.

After I began working at UAB, the university created a development communications team that takes many messages from across campus, tailors them to the audience, captures those audiences with stories, and delivers them in ways that appeal to many readers—donor newsletter features both in print and online, web-based announcements, social media posts, and a variety of other mediums. They address both solicitation marketing and donor recognition pieces showing the ongoing impact of philanthropy. Creative writing is critical to all that they do.

We work closely with the development communications team and university relations so that we are carrying forward appropriate messages. We meet with the development communications team frequently, often daily, to remain in the loop on current messages. These then infuse the various donor relations activities, especially during our current campaign with the tagline, "Give something; change everything." We repeat important messages and concentrate on the five mission pillars of the university: research, education, patient care, community service, and economic development. We also meet regularly with the director of development communications to look ahead at the calendar and projects on the horizon. We discuss how we can promote and facilitate the director's efforts and collaborate with our own.

Hiring Excellent Writers

Although all members of our team must be able to communicate clearly in writing, I put greater emphasis on the particular skill of writing when hiring a stewardship communications specialist versus a stewardship reporting specialist. During an interview for a communications position, writing and proofreading tests are given to all applicants selected.

I ask each applicant to write a letter acknowledging a major gift from Mr. James Donor. The test instructions include a note from the pretend donor saying his gift is in support of diabetes research and is given in honor of his sister, Jane Donor, who has type 1 diabetes, and in memory of his mother, Charity Donor, who passed away from complications of type 2 diabetes. The letter provides a chance to see what type of research a candidate will accomplish in the time allotted and reflects the individual's style at work under pressure. I find it is a fairly good indicator of future success of the chosen candidate. It also allows me to see what level of research and personalization I can expect from the applicant if selected for the job.

In addition to the letter-writing test, I provide a sample report from one of our faculty members for the applicant to proofread. I have purposely chosen a document that was written by a brilliant faculty member for whom English is a second language. The successful candidate will perform above average on punctuation and grammar correction and will go beyond the scope of the assignment to rearrange the document for a more logical read.

These tests have worked for me time and again. I am proud to say that every person I have ever hired has been successful; however, that doesn't mean there weren't some growing pains along the way.

Training Talented Staff to Fit the Job Requirements

There are many good resources for improving writing skills. My training style goes beyond teaching components and begins with a more philosophical approach to behavior and appealing to an individual's ego and psyche. The book *How to Win Friends and Influence People* written by Dale Carnegie was one of the first best-selling self-help books and was published in 1936. I highly recommend it for all to read.

A reading list is included as an appendix to this article, and there are writing workshops available. Although I do not have any to personally recommend, I suggest picking a workshop or class that is specific to the improvement in skill desired. For example, if a person needs improvement in reflecting the impact of gifts, perhaps a storytelling workshop is best, while a more technical grammar and punctuation series (see Media References on page 86 for a TED-Ed recommended series) would be suitable for an individual whose use of commas and sentence structure is sporadic.

One of the most basic things I recommend, that I must admit is rarely used by those to whom I recommend it, is the taking of notes as an individual is telling you what they want to say. Whenever you can capture some of the speaker's own words it will make the writing, whatever it is, more genuine and, therefore, more effective.

Book 1 | June 2016

Required or Elective? The Importance of Creative Writing Skill
to the Practice of Donor Relations and Stewardship

A good writer can enhance the overall reach of a service-based organization and is essential to its ongoing growth and success. Likewise, a poor writer can hurt the organization even with the best of intentions. It is critical for those responsible for donor relations and stewardship to have a good understanding of what creative writing means to success and, in most cases, to also be able to write well in the various styles discussed in this article.

Every organization produces a style guide and this should be in each writer's portfolio. The style guide is usually based on a published style manual. Most organizations elect to use either the *Associated Press Stylebook* or the *Chicago Manual of Style*. There are countless other style manuals that can be reviewed with an Internet search on style manual or manual of style. Other style guides, such as *The Elements of Style*, can be accessed in the same way.

These guides help writers present a consistent voice and way of communicating to readers. Areas of individual style or conflict in usage can be resolved with reference to the style guide. For instance, the question of whether to put one or two spaces after punctuation can be resolved by referring to the style guide. Individual preference succumbs to organizational style.

The organization's style guide can step off from the published manual to include use of the organization's logo, titles, names of departments, etc. Conformity with the style guide is critical to presenting a unified face to the public and reduces confusion as well. Part of the orientation of all employees within the organization should be introduction of the style guide. Writers should be trained and evaluated on their consistent and correct use of the style guide.

We often find ourselves invited by our fundraising colleagues in the units to proofread their correspondence and other writing. We always oblige them and use these occasions as opportunities to spread the word about the style guide and how to use it. We don't expect that these individual efforts will convert all our colleagues, but we are pleased to be invited to help them represent the organization in clear prose that is in line with the style standard.

Our human resources department offers training on writing for the university. Many other organizations probably have training like this as well. I encourage my staff and my colleagues to take advantage of these workshops and other training offered on the Internet, at proprietary workshops, or at conferences like those offered by ADRP, CASE, and AFP.

Conclusion

First and foremost, those of us who work in donor relations and stewardship are communicators. Being able to write well, to express ourselves in words, whether in letters, reports, or in remarks for oral delivery, we serve as proclaimers of the mission of our organizations. We use well-chosen and well-crafted words to connect philanthropists and those who would be philanthropists to our organizations.

Is writing critical to donor relations and stewardship? Writing is the foundation of our practice. There are many styles of writing, from exposition, to creative, to narrative writing. All good writing, however, is interesting to read, and often compelling. Mixing styles to attract and retain the attention of the reader is often necessary, especially in writing for donor relations and stewardship.

If writing is fundamental to donor relations and stewardship, then practitioners have an obligation to prepare themselves to take on the array of assignments and responsibilities that require an excellent command of the various forms of verbal expression. Anyone interested in pursuing a career in donor relations and stewardship might expect to be tested during a job interview to assess the level and quality of skill.

Managers also must be prepared to assess the level of competence of new employees in writing across a range of styles and purposes, from acknowledgment writing to report generation to crafting remarks for speakers at events. Managers themselves must be skilled composers of letters and all forms of executive communications. Keeping and promoting good writers requires thoughtful management of staff and conversations with the organization's leadership about how the institution itself can invest in training and retention of good writers.

Being a good writer entails responsibility beyond the immediate confines of the office of donor relations and stewardship. Promulgating the brand identification tools and style guides of the organization is an important part of management. Reaching out to others across the advancement team to help those who are not strong writers is an obligation, not simply a courtesy. Offering to present staff development workshops or conversations over brown bag lunches makes a difference in elevating the quality of verbal presentation across the fundraising department and the organization.

Daphne B. Powell is the senior director of donor relations and stewardship at the University of Alabama at Birmingham. She developed, implemented, and oversees UAB's comprehensive stewardship program for gift acknowledgment, recognition, and reporting. She is a charter member of and frequent volunteer for the Association of Donor Relations Professionals. Currently, she is chair-elect of the Alabama School of Fine Arts Foundation Board of Directors.

Reading List and Other Resources

References:

Ahern, Tom. *Seeing through a Donor's Eyes: How to Make a Persuasive Case for Everything from Your Annual Drive to Your Planned Giving Program to Your Capital Campaign*. Medfield, Mass.: Emerson & Church Publishers, 2009.

Brooks, Jeff. *The Fundraiser's Guide to Irresistible Communications*. Medfield, Mass.: Emerson & Church Publishers, 2012.

Burk, Penelope. *Donor-Centered Fundraising*. Chicago, Il.: Cygnus Applied Research, Inc., 2003.

Carnegie, Dale. *How to Win Friends and Influence People*. New York, N.Y.: Pocket Books, 1936.

Feinberg, Steven L. (ed.). *Crane's Blue Book of Stationery: The Styles and Etiquette of Letters, Notes, and Invitations*. New York, N.Y.: Crane & Co., 2002.

Frank, Francine Wattman, and Paula A. Treichler. *Language, Gender, and Professional Writing: Theoretical Approaches and Guidelines for Nonsexist Usage*. (1st ed.). New York, N.Y.: Modern Language Association of America: 1989.

Shertzer, Margaret. *The Elements of Grammar*. New York, N.Y.: MacMillan, 1986.

Strunk, William, Jr., and E. B. White. *The Elements of Style*. (4th ed.). New York, N.Y.: Pearson,1999.

Swift, Kate. *The Handbook of Nonsexist Writing: For Writers, Editors and Speakers*. (2nd ed.). Bloomington, Ind.: iUniverse, 2001.

Warwick, Mal. *How to Write Successful Fundraising Appeals*. (3rd ed.). Malden, Mass.: Josey-Bass, 2013.

Wolf, Thomas. *How to Connect with Donors and Double the Money You Raise*. Medfield, Mass.: Emerson & Church Publishers, 2011.

Maggio, Rosalie. *The Dictionary of Bias-Free Usage: A Guide to Nondiscriminatory Language*. Westport, Conn.: Greenwood Publishing Group, 1991.

Media:

TED-Ed Blog: Be a Better Writer in 15 Minutes: 4 TED-Ed lessons on grammar and word choice.

http://blog.ed.ted.com/2014/05/29/be-a-better-writer-in-15-minutes-4-ted-ed-lessons-on-grammar-and-word-choice/

Mary Norris is authoritative, humorous, and insightful in her explanations of "all facets of language."

video.newyorker.com/series/comma-queen

Facebook Daily Tips:

https://www.facebook.com/DailyWritingTips/?fref=ts

https://www.facebook.com/writerscircle/?fref=ts

https://www.facebook.com/grammarly/?fref=ts

https://www.facebook.com/GrammarGirl/?fref=ts

Style Guides:

Associated Press Stylebook

https://www.apstylebook.com/

The Chicago Manual of Style Online

www.chicagomanualofstyle.org/

MLA Style | Modern Language Association

https://www.mla.org/MLA-Style

Institutional style guides:

https://www.uab.edu/brand/home/standards/writing

UAB's brand home provides a complete representation of all the possible areas where design or writing style might pertain. Studying what UAB has compiled in one place will be instructive in determining how your organization might approach the important subject of branding, including design elements and writing style.

http://brand.iu.edu/apply/editorial-style/style-guide/

Indiana University's brand guide is comprehensive. Notice the listing of all outside sources used by IU to determine its style.

http://www.cincinnatichildrens.org/assets/0/78/315/339/42f1df01-d9b4-4774-ac96-7a58a53a4668.pdf

Cincinnati Children's Hospital also publishes its style guide. The range of resources used to compile this guide is different from that used by universities and colleges.

http://www.amnh.org/our-research/scientific-publications/for-authors/style-manual

Style guides like this one for the American Museum of Natural History cover the organization's rules for preparing manuscripts for production and publishing.

http://aspcapro.org/sites/pro/files/aspca_mym_brand_standards_toolbook.pdf

Brand standards toolkits can be whimsical like this one for the ASPC.

Becoming a better writer:

Doherty, Barbara and Charlotte. *Expository Writing: Writing to Explain*. Franklin, N.J.: Educational Impressions, 2002.

LaRoque, Paula. *The Book of Writing: The Ultimate Guide to Writing Well*. Grey and Guvnor Press, 2013.

Felsch, Rudolf. *The Classic Guide to Better Writing: Step-by-Step Techniques and Exercises to Write Simply, Clearly and Correctly*. New York, N.Y.: Collins Reference, 1996.

Grapes, Stephen. *Read This, Write Better: An Unconventional Guide to Becoming an Amazing Writer*. Iowa City, Iowa: The Writing University, 2016.

Wendig, Chuck. *500 Ways to Be a Better Writer*. Terribleminds, 2011

Professionalism in Donor Relations & Stewardship

By Julia S. Emlen

Those of us who practice donor relations and stewardship are pleased to claim the title of professional for our work. Since 2004, we have had the Association of Donor Relations Professionals to validate our claim to it.[1] Still, questions persist about what constitutes the professional dimension of our practice. This article attempts to advance this discussion with a review of literature on what defines professionalism and how theories of professional practice might be applied to donor relations and stewardship. A definition of professional donor relations and stewardship practice is advanced as well as some ideas about how to measure the professionalism of our practice. Ways to advance professional practice through training, which might form the basis for discussion at conferences and meetings to realize a definition of professional practice, are included.

Content:

- Review literature defining professionalism and professional practice
- Advance a definition of professionalism for donor relations and stewardship
- Recommend training to promote the criteria for professionalism
- Introduce a platform for measuring the effectiveness of our practice based on a definition of professionalism

Glossary:

- Commitment and character professionalism: a characterization of professionalism that can be applied to the status of anyone who is competent to practice donor relations and stewardship through training; maintains specific donor relations skills through continuing professional development; commits to an ethical standard of practice; and is dedicated to protecting the philanthropic intentions and interests of the public.

- Compliance systems professionalism: a characterization of professionalism in which the practitioner has experience in all donor relations and stewardship skills and is responsible for collaboration and coordination across the organization to ensure that a philanthropist's gift is used according to any agreement between the philanthropist and the organization. The compliance systems professional seeks to build trust between the philanthropist and the organization. The specific tools used by the compliance systems professional include the organization's mission statement, vision statement, strategic plan, organizational policies and procedures, fundraising plan and gift-acceptance policies and procedures. This practitioner often plays a role in establishing these corporate and governance mechanisms and oversees reporting to donors on gift management.

- Recognition systems professionalism: a characterization of professionalism in which the practitioner has experience in all donor relations and stewardship skills and is responsible for collaboration and coordination across the organization to ensure that a philanthropist is recognized according to any agreement between the philanthropist and the organization in conformance with the organization's recognition practices; and facilitates donor engagement in order to encourage additional and other philanthropy and to convey the appreciation of the organization. The recognition systems professional seeks to deliver the messages of the organization to promote realization of the mission through philanthropy. The specific tools used by the recognition systems professional include the organization's mission statement, vision statement, strategic plan, organizational policies and procedures, fundraising plan and marketing communications strategy. This practitioner often plays a role in establishing these corporate mechanisms and oversees acknowledgment and other forms of recognition and engagement.

Introduction

By what right or from what position or to claim what status do we don the mantle of professionalism? What difference does it make to our work that we consider ourselves professionals or that others see us in that light? In this article, we will review definitions of professionalism; promote a definition of professionalism for our practice in order to circumscribe our profession. The purpose of this exercise is to help us understand the fundamental nature of our work as a profession; to create shared definitions of our work, its sources and legitimacy; to recommend criteria for training in the profession; and to introduce a platform for measuring the effectiveness of our work.

The Literature on Professionalism

Defining professionalism has been of interest to practitioners across a wide spectrum of the traditional (clergy, lawyers, physicians), the skilled (accountants, financial planners, health workers, etc.), and the aspiring (hairdressers, human resource managers, and others who have specific practices that might not yet have been codified into a profession). The idea and ideal of professionalism has been researched by sociologists, educators and others who study the institutionalization of expertise. Through their efforts, they seek to provide a restrictive definition of the concept of professionalism, outline affirming processes to attain professional status and assess the effect on social and economic status conferred by the exclusivity of professionalism.

Early studies by sociologists have done much to define the characteristics of the professional person, from preparation for professional work, to continuing skill refreshment and maintenance required to retain professional status, to the character and temperament of the professional. The oldest of these efforts is probably the work of Ernest Greenwood who wrote about professionalism in the middle of the twentieth century. His succinct list of the attributes of any professional person focuses on "(1) systematic theory, (2) authority, (3) community sanction, (4) ethical codes, and (5) a culture."[2] Many have taken Greenwood's work and applied it to other times and other sets of practitioners.[3] Other authors have sought to refine Greenwood's work by arguing for the pre-eminence of a theoretical basis of practice in defining professionalism;[4] or examining the problems in the entire exercise of defining professionalism or a profession;[5] or focusing on the role of knowledge and expertise in professionalism;[6] or underlining ethics as the foundation of professionalism, essentially opening the arena of professional practice to anyone who operates from a moral as much as from a knowledge base.[7]

Theories of Professionalism and Donor Relations and Stewardship

In all cases, these ideas about professionalism have something to offer practitioners of donor relations and stewardship. In this section, we'll look more closely at some of the theories of professionalism and consider ways in which they might define and promote professionalism in donor relations and stewardship. This discussion proceeds from the most widely applicable definition of professionalism and moves to more complex interpretations of professional practice.

Moving from the simplest to more complex definitions gives us the opportunity to understand the importance of the history of donor relations and stewardship in the pursuit of professional status and also to consider the possibility of identifying levels of professionalism in the practice. Having a scale of professional practice might give us a basis for evaluating the level at which anyone working in donor relations and stewardship is functioning; suggest criteria for training new practitioners; and provide the means for evaluating the condition of any particular donor relations and stewardship program. In these ways, those of us in donor relations and stewardship may develop an understanding of why we engage in certain practices, moving us beyond considering only what we do. We may also better understand how to advance our work within an organization because we have a better grasp of where we are operating relative to the particulars of our practice in relation to the fundraising cycle of an organization.

Character and Commitment Professionals

At its most basic level, professionalism can be applied to those who become competent in their chosen sector through training; maintain their skills through continuing professional development; and commit to ethical behavior, to protect the interests of the public.[8] In this view, professionals include physicians, lawyers, bankers, advisers, financial managers, accountants, donor relations practitioners, healthcare workers, hairdressers, mechanics and many others. Anyone who meets standards of initial and continuing education, who wants to build skills, "solve problems, do good work, and be involved in making decisions which help to improve people's lives" can qualify as a professional because they display character and commitment.[9] A person can pursue professional credentials at any time, at any age, through any number of channels and opportunities, because the foundation of professionalism in this case is intention. Acquiring skills and expertise is a matter of affinity or perhaps the results of an occupational preference test. The skills to be learned and applied are important as well, but the pursuit of specific skills comes from the character of the professional, which is essential.

Professionalism in this respect can lead to enhanced economic position in a career or business. In the case of TotalProfessions. com, for example, a group of career developers has captured an idea of professionalism to promote job hunting and preparation for the sometimes arduous work involved in finding a job. One might call this open-door professionalism.

The character and commitment definition probably best defines the professionalism of donor relations and stewardship in its approximately thirty-year history as a separate category of work within advancement and fundraising. This field has attracted practitioners who have the personal traits of commitment and character, which might encompass institutional history, personality and work ethic.[10] Commitment might further be defined in this case as having knowledge of the donors through contacts outside advancement; having a sense of decorum in dealing with sensitive information; and having the trust of executives and administrators as someone who is discreet and meticulous. Perhaps fundamental to this approach is the impression that donor relations and stewardship are "just good manners."

The character and commitment approach to professionalism overall, and in the case of donor relations and stewardship, does not preclude expertise and training. As the early history of donor relations and stewardship attests, even before the founding of the Association of Donor Relations and Stewardship (ADRP), early practitioners often reached out to one another for advice about how to acknowledge donors, how to write good letters, how to accumulate information in databases, or how to welcome donors to meet those whom their philanthropy supports.

In the 1990s, the New England Stewardship Conference was an outgrowth of that interest and commitment to understanding better ways to provide donor relations and stewardship services to donors across the philanthropic spectrum. ADRP maintains and has published a document of elements or principles of donor relations (see Appendix 2) which is the work of early leaders of the association, especially Nancy Lubich McKinney.[11] This outline of the fundamental skills and the areas of their application form an excellent guide for developing a set of skills that the donor relations and stewardship practitioner must have.[12]

Current definitions of professional practice in donor relations and stewardship may continue to reside largely in this conceptualization: character and commitment. This might be the result of bureaucratic categorizations of positions according to human-resource criteria that determine placement and remuneration within an organization. A review of conference programs confirms the effort to promote the skills which underpin donor relations and stewardship and identify how to best practice those skills. This is an effort to secure the expertise that has grown from initial character and commitment professionalism. Salary and job title surveys demonstrate the effort to bring back from conferences to the organizations where we work what has been learned in order to advance our positions as professional workers, elevate our status and increase our salaries.

In the last decade, conferences have included workshops on professional advancement and any survey of the job titles associated with working in donor relations and stewardship reveals that there is upward mobility. The position content descriptions of anyone from assistant/associate director through vice chancellor, however, may not reflect specific expertise or knowledge in donor relations and stewardship as much as executive skill or experience, although differentiation of the tasks—what we do, from acknowledgment to compliance management to event planning and report writing—also plays a role in our growth within bureaucratic organizations.

As a matter of fact, what may be developing is a professional class of managers and executives who can oversee process and production, often the basis of donor relations and stewardship practice, but who may not have themselves specific donor relations and stewardship expertise or who have not worked in donor relations and stewardship roles before becoming managers of this work.

The number of managers and executives overseeing donor relations and stewardship operations who do not have direct experience in the practice is witness to the fact that a good manager may be considered by executive leaders as effective in supervising donor relations and stewardship services within an organization. Gift officers who move into management of donor relations and stewardship operations may reflect a preference by executives for leaders with solicitation experience. It would be interesting to see if the migration goes the other way as well, with seasoned donor relations and stewardship officers, with experience in compliance management and recognition, taking on major gift officer roles with success.

Professional managers and executives, regardless of their backgrounds, can promote the professional status of those who function at the commitment and character level of professionalism in donor relations and stewardship. These managers have budgeting responsibility and outcome accountability that can help tie the production and processes of donor relations and stewardship practice back to greater success in solicitations by gift officers. As administrators, these managers must account for the return on the investment of the organization in donor relations and stewardship activities. It is in the interest of the organization and the purview of the executives to define and fund what moves donors to their highest level of philanthropy. As a result, these management professionals may promote the growth of knowledge and expertise in donor relations and stewardship practice by demanding a strategic basis for any particular activity carried out in the name of donor relations and stewardship.

A more rigorous strategic approach may in time overwhelm the "it's-just-good-manners" mantra about donor relations and stewardship. When this happens, donor relations and stewardship practice will turn on the question of why we do something rather than how an activity or task is done. It remains to be seen how this process will ensue because testing donor relations and stewardship practices remains difficult, and tradition as a reason for continuing common practices is strong. Managers and executives who question why a practice is good manners and further why good manners make a difference in philanthropy can move our practice along. It may be this class of managers without prior experience in donor relations and stewardship who can ask these questions.

Systems Professionals

The commitment and character definition of professionalism stresses production of particular products in particular ways. Another view of professionalism within donor relations and stewardship might be in terms of systems management as the professional work overseeing production management.

In the 1990s, GE applied the principles of Six Sigma to redirect responsibility for excellence from quality-management professionals to the production units within the company.[13] Assurance of the quality of product and process, from manufacturing to marketing to sales, was redistributed from a separate unit dedicated to managing quality to the areas of production (manufacture, marketing, sales, etc.). Quality, went the reasoning, was the business of the producers who were closest to the product, not of reviewers who conducted their review of quality from a distance and at the end of production.

Unfortunately, assigning the management of quality to the production team failed to reduce errors. It proved no better in promoting excellence than former quality-management teams which operated as traditional, inspection-oriented after-the-fact monitors. A quality-management unit viewed a defective part after a failure in production, adding no value to the process and creating remedies with perhaps limited applicability across the production cycle. A defect was not analyzed in terms of its occurrence within a larger process but at a moment in time.

GE and other companies applied the Six Sigma standard as a result of these failures.[14] A new quality systems-management team evolved from the question, "who owns quality, those who produce the goods or those who assure the quality of the goods." Six Sigma analysis revealed that everyone owned quality, so the systems professional supersedes the quality manager and works across the organization with all phases of production, from engineering and design, to production, to sales.

What role, then, do the former quality police have in this system? They may lose their status as experts in particular activities that assess defective production, but they take on the role of coordinators and facilitators to advance quality across the organization and in real time. A set of responsibilities and skills have developed from this transition, including convening the quality producers and engaging them with other quality centers, including marketing and sales. They have become instructors, helping production managers inculcate the value of quality within each employee's work. They have acted as reporters of the effects of quality management. Their role has evolved into four basic areas:

- Ensuring proper and periodic training on aspects of quality production

- Performing tests to calibrate machinery and measure consistency

- Managing testing and handling equipment issues

- Controlling the quality manual and its use

As a result, the elements of quality across the organization, rather than the production of quality within a unit, become the work of the quality systems professional. Managing the elements of the quality system aggregates to this team rather than to managers overseeing quality at various steps in production. This role is also more immune to the ups and downs of corporate fortunes than the latter because the quality systems professional has a role in ensuring quality, not simply noting its failure. The organizational value from identifying and deploying a quality systems professional is clear:

- A smaller team is needed

- Quality becomes an institutional value, supported from the highest executive levels

- Interconnections between quality centers can be linked by the quality professional

- The knowledge base and expertise of the quality professional are clearly defined

- Problems are identified through planning and evaluation, leading to better practices

- Only those practices that promote the desired outcome are promoted

Systems Management and Donor Relations and Stewardship

The systems management professional approach to donor relations and stewardship takes us beyond the character and commitment approach in our professional practice which was described in the previous section.

We begin to focus on elements of our work that are perhaps analogous to the production elements of GE or Motorola: gift agreements and compliance; acknowledgment; recognition and engagement. Instead of functioning in a single department, however, we reach out to colleagues across the organization to link their work with the goal of promoting philanthropy. Many of our internal goals in donor relations and stewardship might fall away in this model as we become more attached to the strategic direction and mission of the organization in formulating and establishing our donor relations and stewardship practice and more sensitive to accountability for increasing philanthropy. Here lies territory for developing measurements of efficiency and effectiveness.

Systems Management and Compliance Management

We might equate the production on the shop floor to our efforts to assure or manage compliance with gift agreements, which represents an important and often complicated aspect of donor relations and stewardship. We must reach out to various organizational partners as well as engage with gift officers to influence gift-agreement generation in order to ensure compliance with donor intentions. We might also have a role in training gift officers in ways to avoid unrealistic criteria and explaining the limits of the organization's resources to meet a donor's expectations. These efforts go to the heart of the trust we hope to engender in our supporters by adhering to gift agreements.

At this time, much of our compliance-management efforts are centered on making sure that gift criteria are met. There is much we can do, however, to serve as systems management professionals in securing compliance. As with GE's experience, we might start with a compliance management working group that looks at the influence of core institutional factors, such as the mission, vision and strategic direction of the institution, through gift-agreement development, gift-officer training in their use, and application. The focus on compliance systems management will have a historical aspect as well because older or evolving organizations look back at the history of their fidelity to expressed donor intentions and make amends for lapses, or use them to advise and direct current practices.

This effort may bring us to a different application of the concept of donor-centered fundraising. We may become more proficient at promoting the message inherent in the organization's mission to find synchrony with the philanthropic interests of the donor. In this way we reach out to prospects and donors with a message that can attract the philanthropic intentions and interests of the prospect and donor, rather than trying to find donor interests within the organization. This effort may help us separate compliance from recognition as well, giving us greater leeway in determining how to recognize and engage our donors and perhaps simplifying recognition.

The compliance systems manager may also serve as the ambassador across the organization so that donor relations and stewardship become institutional priorities. The roles carried out by the systems management professionals at GE may be slightly revised to describe the work of this important donor relations and stewardship practitioner:

- Convening an institutional compliance working group to review the components of compliance management, from mission to vision to strategic, fundraising plan

- Developing gift-agreement templates and training on their implementation; testing their use and revising and retraining as needed

- Reviewing and revising gift-acceptance policies and procedures to simplify compliance and separate it from recognition and engagement

- Convening solicitation staff for training in conversations with donors that promote an understanding of how the organization uses gifts, in order to forestall compliance-management issues

- Reviewing older agreements and bringing institutional practice into line

- Controlling the compliance manual and its use

Articulating compliance systems management as an element of donor relations and stewardship is an important step in understanding a range of issues faced in our work. First and foremost is concern for who does the work of reconciling gift-agreement details versus the other types of work typical of this practice, including reporting, recognition management, and engagement which require different sets of skills.[15]

Recognizing the importance of compliance management as a process extending from mission to agreement implementation to gift-officer training also gives sufficient range to the work of a donor relations and stewardship staff member to qualify as systems management professionalism.[16] The opportunity to develop expertise, skill and knowledge exists as well. Organizing a compliance-management working group would require endorsement from the highest level of the organization, an important factor in advancing the position of the donor relations and stewardship practitioner within the organization. Setting standards and maintaining their governance as a means of establishing donor relations and stewardship as an institutional priority becomes a professional function within the institution.

Systems Management and Donor Relations

At the same time, we are seeing greater interest among donor relations and stewardship practitioners in message delivery systems. Initially this was represented by traditional written communications and social events, but today it includes social media, video production and an array of donor recognition devices and events.

There are story tellers among us whose outlook on the world is different from that of the compliance managers, but whose role is equally critical in promoting the values of the institution among our supporters. Just as much as the compliance systems manager functions as a professional in building trust in the institution, the donor recognition systems manager serves to deliver the message, again from the mission, through the vision, with the strategic direction influencing choices of messages and the communications and fundraising plans which inform the methods and determine the constituency addressed.

A recognition management working group is just as important in organizing these efforts to deliver the message of the organization as the compliance management working group is essential to ensuring the realization of donors' intentions. Executive sanction must pertain. Opportunities to develop expertise, knowledge of the applications to donors within a specific organization is important, and the range of operation is broad. The recognition systems manager becomes a professional in a different and complementary capacity to the compliance systems manager. Both roles spring from donor relations and stewardship, but track in different directions.

Like the compliance systems manager, the recognition systems manager may serve as an ambassador within the organization to promote the priority status of donor relations and stewardship in the following ways:

- Convening an institutional recognition working group to review the components of recognition and recognition management, from mission to vision to strategic, fundraising and communications plans

- Developing messages based on the communications plan and identifying constituencies and segments to reach, as well as methods for message delivery

- Reviewing and revising message delivery systems to promote philanthropic response from prospects and donors

- Establishing metrics and points of measurement to determine the success of recognition and engagement

- Convening solicitation staff for training in message delivery which promotes an understanding of the mission of the organization

Creating and Managing the Professional Spectrum of Stewardship and Donor Relations

Coming into the mix of professionalism and its definition for donor relations and stewardship are a number of attributes which may include the following:

1. Possessing skill in writing, project management and interpersonal skills to implement elements of practice including gift-acceptance and compliance management,

acknowledgment, recognition, reporting, and engagement planning and management[17]

2. Having experience in financial management, personnel management, strategic planning, executive leadership

3. Understanding and managing organizational complexity and attendant centralization or decentralization of advancement and the number and distribution of the donor relations and stewardship staff; specialization or all-encompassing services

4. Comprehending the mission and scope of the organization and its resources to implement the mission

5. Identifying and deploying internal and external resources available for production

6. Seizing and/or creating opportunities for professional development and career advancement

7. Seeking professional advancement or seeking to decelerate from advanced professional standing

With this list, we might formulate an understanding of the nature of donor relations and stewardship professionalism within any particular organization. The following are offered as examples with the realization that there are multiple permutations of these combinations.

1. Small, centralized—may refer to an organization in one location with a directed, focused mission, with programs and services delivered to a defined group; all resources centrally housed, although possibly unitized, and available to everyone. The donor relations practitioner must know how to manage all elements of the donor relations and stewardship program, including reaching out to specialized units for support on certain projects. The focus may be on compliance, reporting and acknowledgment, with recognition and engagement conceptualized and planned within the small shop, but supported and managed in collaboration with staff members in

other departments. The small, centralized configuration may be managed by the commitment and character professional.

2. Small, decentralized—may describe a new donor relations and stewardship program emerging within a central advancement department serving the decentralized divisions or departments of the organization. The donor relations practitioner may function much as described above, with knowledge of how to manage all elements of the donor relations and stewardship program. This configuration may require central management of gift agreements and management and coordination of acknowledgment. Recognition and engagement, however, become functions of the separate departments, with limited project management assistance from the small shop.

This effort may be managed by the commitment and character professional who is beginning to acquire advanced skills through training or education; or may be a veteran commitment and character professional who is seeking new opportunities and may have to acquire additional expertise through education for career advancement; or may be a late-career donor relations and stewardship professional who is looking for the opportunity to return to production-based practice.

3. Large, centralized—may evolve in a larger organization that retains a central advancement office, but because of special initiatives, the donor relations and stewardship office must add staff to provide services; or the organization is differentiating and changes in the configuration of the advancement effort are part of the planning. This shop may be experiencing the beginnings of differentiation or specialization of donor relations and stewardship work, with dedicated acknowledgment and report writers and perhaps gift-agreement and management staff, as well as events managers overseeing recognition and engagement.

This shop may begin with the type of leadership described in the small, centralized office, under the direction of a character/ commitment professional who is a skilled donor relations and stewardship practitioner with many years of experience, but has no formal training or experience in executive leadership. Over time, this office will need management by an experienced leader with an extensive background in donor relations and stewardship or an advanced degree and specialization in executive leadership. Ideally, the leader would be a systems management professional and the choice of compliance systems professional or recognition systems professional may depend on the condition of the program as it emerges. If this leader does not have donor relations and stewardship skills (gift acceptance and management; acknowledgment; recognition; reporting; and engagement) this leader may have to reach back to acquire skills in donor relations and stewardship.

4. Large, decentralized—this configuration may describe donor relations and stewardship offered in a national or international organization with many offices and departments in different locations; or an organization with one location but many divisions; or perhaps an organization differentiating its divisions into centers and cross-disciplinary offices that are beginning to fundraise.

   This shop is most likely to need a professional with skills in the elements of donor relations and stewardship and advanced executive leadership credentials and years of experience. This leader probably has emerged from years in donor relations and stewardship practice and is called upon in this shop to serve as a systems manager.

   Depending on the needs of the organization, this leader may be skilled in compliance systems management or recognition systems management. This office may require deputy leaders who take on separate roles in compliance systems management and recognition systems management under an executive leader.

   This configuration is likely to be one that emerges more often over the decades as nonprofit organizations become more complex. Leaders in donor relations and stewardship who are concerned about the development of the field as a profession might want to focus on this model as a means of studying how to assist in their formulation and how to determine the best ways to provide professional development and designate career paths to this type of professional practice that will require both extensive skills and expertise and leadership capacity.

These four models are but a few of the configurations possible and likely in donor relations and stewardship. We can gather from them, however, a sense of the influence of a working definition of professionalism in donor relations and stewardship on recruitment, training, education, and career development opportunities and imperatives. We can also understand how our professional leaders might be of assistance to organizations as they attempt to secure best practices in donor relations and stewardship.

These models give us a platform from which to audit our own donor relations and stewardship efforts to determine what our staffing needs might be and the type of professional we are seeking. We might also use these configurations to help us build certification programs managed through an association or educational institution. Having these definitions and structural examples helps us develop measures of efficiency and effectiveness. They also give executive leaders the opportunity to predict and staff or develop their donor relations and stewardship programs.

Fundamental to these efforts is a recognition of three discrete types of professionalism. There is play among these categories as the character and commitment professional takes on management duties, thereby stepping into the systems professional role or roles.

1. Character and commitment professionalism—skill in the elements of donor relations and stewardship, gift-agreement and compliance management, acknowledgment, reporting, recognizing and engaging

2. Compliance systems professionalism—skill in all areas but focusing on gift-agreement and compliance management and reporting and responsible for synchronizing the resources of the organization and its principles and practices (from mission through policy and procedures and all types of strategic planning) to realize the mission through philanthropy

3. Recognition systems professionalism—skill in all areas but focusing on acknowledgment, recognition and engagement, and responsible for synchronizing the resources of the organization and its principles and practices (from mission through policy and procedures and all types of strategic planning) to realize the mission through philanthropy

What Makes a Professional a Professional

Even given the preceding two working descriptions of professionalism in donor relations and stewardship—commitment and character and systems management professionalism—we must define the concept of professionalism and apply it to donor relations and stewardship. Being professional has important ramifications for us in society as much as it does in our work and among our colleagues. Status is important and being considered a professional is an essential component of it.

Going back to basics can help us develop a fundamental sense of donor relations and stewardship as a profession. For this review, we look more closely at Greenwood's article on the attributes of a profession. As he notes, sociologists define a profession as "an organized group which is constantly interacting with the society that forms its matrix, which performs its social functions through a network of formal and informal relationships, and which creates its own subculture requiring adjustments to it as a prerequisite for career success."[18]

In 1957, Greenwood cited the United States Census Bureau's professional category in its occupational classifications as "accountant, architect, artist, attorney, clergyman, college professor, dentist, engineer, journalist, judge, librarian, natural scientist, optometrist, pharmacist, physician, social scientist, social worker, surgeon, and teacher."[19] Things have changed, however, since Greenwood considered the issue of professionalism, and the U.S. Census Bureau now lists 539 specific occupational categories arranged in 23 occupational groups, within which professionals are incorporated depending on the work performed, skills, education, training, and the credentials of the practitioner.[20]

There is room to include donor relations and stewardship professionals within the classification of professional, perhaps with less assistance from our government friends. The openness of the government's classification system reflects back to both our initial character and commitment definition of professionalism as well as our systems manager professional definition.

Greenwood's list of five characteristics of a profession, however, continues to hold value and has been referenced in many discussions of professionalism in today's literature, referenced in this article and considered at greater length below for this discussion. Greenwood sees professionalism along a continuum and the degree of professionalism reflects a greater or lesser quantity of these qualities.

Systematic Body of Theory

Greenwood acknowledges the traditional consideration of the difficulty of the work of the professional, the mastery required through education and practice, as a hallmark of the professional over the nonprofessional occupations. He suggests, however, that a theoretical base from which the professional operates is equally important. The uniqueness of the practice shares equal status with the expertise and skill required.

Does the practice of donor relations and stewardship require a unique theoretical base or significant mastery? It would be an interesting exercise to gather information on the preparation of those involved in donor relations and stewardship to see what consistency there might be in the educational preparation of these practitioners. There is most likely to be little or none. It might also be interesting to attempt to correlate workshops attended, webinars viewed, or courses taken to the position and professional progress from one type of professionalism to another.

This state of affairs supports the commitment-character concept of professionalism. Many practitioners have migrated to positions in donor relations and stewardship because of their closeness to fundraising executives, a position from which they can carry out various functions associated with donor relations and stewardship, as such drafting letters, arranging events, etc.; or because of their interest in nurturing donor relationships within the organization. There will always be a role for this kind of professional and many organizations will promote likely candidates from within to satisfy the need to solve problems and maintain a welcoming face for the organization.

In larger and more complex organizations, the systems manager professional approach may find its way to describe the work of donor relations and stewardship practitioners. The rise of programs training fundraising and philanthropy professionals may also lead to greater theoretical articulation of this work. It will be incumbent upon the profession's leaders to seek and create these opportunities.

To develop a systematic body of theory for donor relations and stewardship, it might be important to abandon the terms donor relations and stewardship, in favor of character/committed practice, compliance systems management and recognition systems management. The terms donor relations and stewardship are now associated with a particular unit, group, or individual within an organization, but the portfolio managed by these people is diffuse and often defined in the moment. Donor relations and stewardship as concepts can be renewed as outcomes of the practices involved in compliance systems management and recognition systems management, both under the mantle of systems professionals. The same is true of the work of the character/committed professional who seeks to promote the outcomes of donor relations and stewardship through focused work.

Simon Sinek and Kathleen A. Kelly can help us stage our systematic body of theory in a way that encompasses the tasks most often associated with donor relations and stewardship in a framework that begins with a statement of purpose ahead of statements of function. This schematic includes Sinek's golden circles and Kelley's stewardship behaviors and finally the ADRP elements of donor relations.

Why?[21]	To advance the institutions mission by bringing our donors and prospects to their highest level of philanthropy			
How?[22]	Reciprocity	Responsibility	Reporting	Relationship Nurturing
What?[23]	Receipting, Acknowledgment, Recognition	Gift-agreements, Compliance	Compliance, Recognition	Recognition, Engagement

The opportunity to specify the donor relations and stewardship outcomes desired by an institution and in relation to a particular fundraising initiative or cycle remains. For example, a small, centralized organization might want an emphasis on recognition and engagement during a campaign. An emerging organization may want to figure out how to coordinate as efficiently as possible issues of compliance management. Donor relations and stewardship outcomes sought or organizational status and strategic direction can help determine the type of professional or the configuration of professional practice required. We might get closer to understanding how the systems management professional operates, either in compliance or recognition, through study of stewardship working groups,[24] which have emerged in many organizations as a way to identify and solve donor relations and stewardship issues.

Developing the skills and expertise in each systems management professional category can become part of the work of the existing professional associations and the combined body of practitioners. The inclination in either direction is already at play; it is just a matter of creating the taxonomy. Following from this can be the training and certification appropriate for the practice.

Professional Authority

Greenwood acknowledges that authority derives from the theoretical base of the profession. In the case of most professions, authority is exercised in relation to a client or customer who interacts with the professional to gain from that theoretical knowledge, thereby giving the professional authority in the relationship. The issue of authority looms large for many in donor relations and stewardship because the definition of either term is left to the entity seeking the service, not to the person offering it. Authority is granted by the institution the practitioner serves, not the client or customer, which in this situation would be the donors.

Advancing authority has begun with the promotion of practitioners to higher executive levels within organizations. The span of control exercised by these executives also helps secure greater authority for all practitioners. Again, however, moving away from the terms donor relations and stewardship as activities and defining them as outcomes and goals while moving to more descriptive terms within systems management may pave the way to a greater and more secure level of professional authority.

Even so, the authority of the practitioner is vested by the organization rather than by the donor. Even if the character/commitment professional or the compliance systems professional or the recognition systems professional moved out of the traditional nonprofit setting to a financial management organization offering donor-advised funds, the relationship would still be with the donor only on behalf of the institution.

To achieve the state of greater authority, character/commitment professionals, compliance systems professionals and recognition systems professionals would have to be promoted into executive positions, which now are frequently taken by professional managers who may not have expertise in donor relations and stewardship. A pathway to greater authority might be accomplished by securing credentials in management (MBAs; MPAs) or gaining experience in solicitation work as a major gift officer.

Community Sanction

When the profession can demonstrate its control over its knowledge through accreditation, it will be granted community sanction. In addition, community sanction means that the knowledge and expertise are not subject to second judgment by the community. Neither condition currently applies for those who practice donor relations and stewardship. Creating accreditation in the basic elements of donor relations or in the skills of compliance management and recognition management as systems professions could help move the process of codifying professional skill and build community sanction, not just of the specific actions of a donor relations or stewardship professional, but of specific outcomes produced by the entire nonprofit system.

Ethical Codes

The conduct of any professional who claims special knowledge and certification cannot be compromised if the professionals follow an ethical code of behavior. The Donor Bill of Rights (see Appendix 1) is the document that most likely gives donor relations and stewardship its moral stance within the community. Many others in advancement and fundraising claim this code as their shield and having this blanket across a larger group maintains cooperation, equality, and mutual support that might otherwise fracture as distinct codes of conduct are applied. Donor relations and stewardship practitioners may reflect their efforts to accomplish their outcomes against the statements of the Donor Bill of Rights. Within the practice, specific statements may lend themselves more to one systems management professional or another, but the entire professional practice of character/commitment, compliance systems management and recognition systems management abides by the ethical code provided by the Donor Bill of Rights.

A Culture

Donor relations and stewardship practitioners operate within the organizational subsystem of advancement or development or whatever descriptors are used to define fundraising. Their scope reaches beyond the immediate environment to the world of prospects and donors as well. Further out, practitioners connect across organizations at professional meetings and through their professional associations. Beyond these are small groups of practitioners who congregate as practitioners of the same profession but seek some special consideration or initiative such as regional meetings or discussions among specialized institutions (such as health care versus museum versus animal shelters, etc.) The social value within these groupings is the promotion and validation of the profession and the inculcation of these values among those new to the profession.

Donor relations and stewardship practitioners excel at creating, promoting and maintaining their culture through networks and associations that emerge from the nature of the practice, that is in sharing ideas and working through processes with colleagues. While the practitioners have been successful in expanding their influence and numbers, they have not necessarily been able to elevate the position of the profession across the fundraising world. Training remains task-based and opportunities to forge new ideas and attract new leaders who might build the professional identity have not emerged.

Creating the culture of donor relations and stewardship professionalism is an important task for the practitioners. Next steps in this process might be the formation of a task force to further examine the definitions of professionalism advanced in this article. Initially, and probably for years to come, various definitions may co-exist. Describing the two roles—character and commitment and systems management professionals—including core functions and training, might be first steps. Entry in the profession may come from either direction, eventually depending on experience and certification. Following progress of those who are certified in their professional careers, monitoring the effect of their work on the growth of philanthropy, and developing professional opportunities are possibilities in the future.

A Definition of Donor Relations and Stewardship

Speculation about definitions of donor relations and stewardship professionalism are incomplete without a definition of the field in which the professionals practice. The following is an effort to concatenate all the aspects of the practice discussed in this article in a single mission statement.

Donor relations and stewardship are the outcome of activities that promote the highest levels of philanthropy to the important humanistic causes around the world represented in the work of nonprofit organizations.

Donor relations is the outcome of donor-based activities that derive from the mission and vision, the strategic plan, fundraising plan and communications strategy. Donor relations activities promote management of the relationship with the donor and spread the messages of the organization to those who would engage or enhance their philanthropy to it. Donor relations focuses on donor recognition and engagement, whether through, acknowledgment, events, publications, or other message-delivery activities. Its major activity is recognition management and recognition management systems professionals operate across the organization through the recognition management working group.

Stewardship is the outcome of gift-based activities that promote trust in the organization, and from the mission and vision, the strategic plan, fundraising plan, gift policies and procedures, and reporting. Its major activity is compliance management and compliance management systems professionals operate across the organization through the compliance management working group.

Compliance management and recognition management systems professionals operate within the ethical guidelines provided by the Donor Bill of Rights.

Conclusion

This article attempts to find a basis for declaring donor relations and stewardship to be a profession. Two theories of professionalism are provided. A character and commitment model reflects on the history of donor relations and stewardship which emerged from the growth of advancement over the past thirty years. A systems management professional model emerges from production management work over the same period of time using the Six Sigma model. The former model usually operates within a unit or department and focuses on task-based activities and is more transactional in its scope. The systems management model operates above the unit, reaching across the organization to create value from the work of all in synchrony with the goal of advancing philanthropy. No matter what the professional configuration, donor relations and stewardship professionals seek to advance the mission of the organization through philanthropy and direct their efforts to bringing donors to their highest level of philanthropy.

Much work remains to be done to evaluate these models of professionalism and to carry them forward through the professional concepts developed by sociologists interested in the regulation of expertise. Some suggestions about how to proceed have been advanced and task forces or working groups of practitioners are recommended to begin this work.

The opportunity and imperative to organize training, skills development, and career enhancement cannot be understated. Taking Greenwood's five concepts of the professional and working to make them part of our practice is a worthy, important and critical next step in our development.

Julia S. Emlen is the executive editor of the *Journal of Donor Relations and Stewardship*. She is the principal of Julia S. Emlen Associates and the author of *Intentional Stewardship: Bringing Your Donors to Their Highest Level of Philanthropy*. She serves as the director of scholarships and stewardship at Johnson & Wales University and is an active member of the Association of Donor Relations Professionals.

Endnotes

[1] For the history of ADRP, see www.adrp.net/history.

[2] Greenwood, Ernest. Attributes of a Profession. *Social Work*. July 1957. pp. 45-55.

[3] Abbott, Andrew. *Chaos of Disciplines*. Chicago: University of Chicago Press, 2001.

Abbott, Andrew. *The System of Professions: An Essay on the Division of Expert Labor* Chicago: The University of Chicago Press, 1988.

Freidson, Eliot. *Professional Powers: A Study of the Institutionalization of Formal Knowledge*. Chicago: The University of Chicago Press, 1986.

Freidson, Eliot. *Professionalism: The Third Logic*. Chicago: The University of Chicago Press, 2001.

Brint, Steven. *In an Age of Experts: The Changing Role of Professionals in Politics and Public Life*. Princeton, N.J.: Princeton University Press, 1994.

[4] Hubbard, Susan. *Professionalism versus Practitioner: Making the Case for Theory*. http://orange.eserver.org/issues/3-1/hubbard/html. pp. 1-7.

[5] Cogan, Morris L. The Problem of Defining a Profession. *The Annals of the American Academy of Political and Social Science*. January 1955. Vol. 297; No. 1; pp. 105-111.

[6] Saks, Mike. Defining a Profession: The Role of Knowledge and Expertise. *Professions & Professionalism*. http://urn.nb.no/URN:NBN;no-30970. pp. 1-10.

[7] Sercombe, Howard. Ethics and the idea of a profession. *In Youth Work Ethics*. London: Sage Publications Ltd., 2010. pp. 7-15.

[8] Totalprofessions.com.

[9] Ibid.

[10] Emlen, Julia S. *Intentional Stewardship: Bringing Your Donors to Their Highest Level of Philanthropy*. Washington, D.C.: CASE, 2007.

[11] Nancy Lubich McKinney, "Stewardship in a Decentralized Fundraising Environment," *Intentional Stewardship*, pp. 131-146.

[12] See Nancy Lubich McKinney's interview on page 113 for a discussion of the effect of unit size and distribution on donor relations and stewardship practice.

[13] Hoerl, Roger W. Six Sigma and the Future of the Quality Profession. *Quality Progress*. June 1998. pp. 35-42.

[14] Developed in 1986 by Motorola, Six Sigma is a business management strategy used in many industries to improve the quality of products and services through the removal of defects and errors. The Six Sigma approach involves the creation of work groups representing all areas involved in production in an effort to promote quality.

[15] See blog post, "What Difference Does It Make? Stewardship Versus Donor Relations," ADRP, *The Hub*, January, 2015.

[16] See blog post, "Compliance and Its Role in Stewardship and Donor Relations," ADRP, *The Hub*, April, 2015.

[17] See ADRP Elements of Donor Relations.

[18] Greenwood, p. 45.

[19] Ibid.

[20] http://www.census.gov/people/io/about/occupation.html.

[21] Sinek, Simon. Start with Why—How Great Leaders Inspire Action. TEDx Puget Sound. youtube.com.

[22] Kelly, Kathleen S. *Effective Fund-Raising Management*. New York: Lawrence Erlbaum Associates, Inc., 1998.

[23] ADRP ibid

[24] Emlen, Ibid.

References

Abbott, Andrew. *Chaos of Disciplines*. Chicago: University of Chicago Press, 2001.

Abbott, Andrew. *The System of Professions: An Essay on the Division of Expert Labor*. Chicago: The University of Chicago Press, 1988.

Adams, Tracey L. Profession: A Useful Concept for Sociological Analysis? *Canadian Review of Sociology/Revue canadienne de sociologie*. pp. 49-70.

Brint, Steven. *In an Age of Experts: The Changing Role of Professionals in Politics and Public Life*. Princeton, N.J.: Princeton University Press, 1994.

Cogan, Morris L. The Problem of Defining a Profession. *The Annals of the American Academy of Political and Social Science*. January 1955. Vol. 297; No. 1; pp. 105-111.

Emlen, Julia S. *Intentional Stewardship: Bringing Your Donors to Their Highest Level of Philanthropy*. Washington, D.C.: CASE, 2007.

Freidson, Eliot. *Professional Powers: A Study of the Institutionalization of Formal Knowledge*. Chicago: The University of Chicago Press, 1986.

Freidson, Eliot. *Professionalism: The Third Logic*. Chicago: The University of Chicago Press, 2001.

Greenwood, Ernest. Attributes of a Profession. *Social Work*. July 1957. pp. 45-55.

Hoerl, Roger W. Six Sigma and the Future of the Quality Profession. *Quality Progress*. June 1998. pp. 35-42.

Hubbard, Susan. *Professionalism versus Practitioner: Making the Case for Theory*.

http://orange.eserver.org/issues/3-1/hubbard/html. pp. 1-7.

Kelly, Kathleen S. *Effective Fund-Raising Management*. New York: Lawrence Erlbaum Associates, Inc., 1998.

Saks, Mike. Defining a Profession: The Role of Knowledge and Expertise. *Professions & Professionalism*. http://urn.nb.no/URN:NBN;no-30970. pp. 1-10.

Sercombe, Howard. Ethics and the idea of a profession. *In Youth Work Ethics*. London: Sage Publications Ltd., 2010. pp. 7-15.

Sinek, Simon. Start with Why—How Great Leaders Inspire Action. TEDx Puget Sound. youtube.com.

TotalProfessions.com. What is a Profession?

Wideman, Max. The Attributes of a Profession. maxwideman.com/papers/spectrum/attributes.htm.

The Role of Shop Size and Configuration in Providing Donor Relations Services

An interview with Nancy Lubich McKinney

Editors Julia Emlen and Anne Manner-McLarty had the opportunity to talk with Nancy Lubich McKinney, executive director of donor and gift services at the University of California, Berkeley, and president of the Association of Donor Relations Professionals (ADRP) from 2009 to 2014. We discussed large versus small shops and centralized versus decentralized operations. Our conversation was wide ranging and we're pleased to present our questions and her responses.

The comparison of centralized versus decentralized donor relations and stewardship shops has been a focus for you for many years. What brought you to study the field from this perspective and what has been your experience?

Originally my comparison of the workings of centralized and decentralized donor relations services was just about learning the landscape. I was the first person to hold the donor relations and stewardship position in the central development office at UC Berkeley, and I had the opportunity to create the role and envision our shop's responsibilities within the university. We work from a central position in a distinctly decentralized organization. I needed to know how it was done elsewhere, especially in large organizations like UC Berkeley.

As I look back on my transition from a position in the commercial banking world to my role as director of donor stewardship and then executive director of donor and gift services at UC Berkeley, I am aware of how much my position in the for-profit sector is similar to and has influenced my thinking about donor relations and stewardship. While the fundamental nature of the work is different, there are many parallels. I spent much of my time with the bank coordinating compliance and risk management requirements across many divisions. I managed a small team that grew over the years to a larger group carrying out this important reporting work. From the central office, I provided data and analysis, but I relied on thirty lines of business to make up the comprehensive report every quarter. I had no power over those thirty people who represented the divisions about which we were preparing the report.

Having to get to know the workings of thirty lines of business, get along with everyone, operate with no leverage, and pull it all together within a limited amount of time isn't unlike what I do at UC Berkeley between the central office and the decentralized fundraising departments. The skills I must bring to bear in donor relations and stewardship are business skills. In any area of advancement services you must have good critical thinking skills, be able to think both analytically and creatively. You have to have influence skills and emotional intelligence. I had to gain the participation of my colleagues across the organization to succeed. We accomplished this by demonstrating that the central team could manage the project or program with greater consistency and efficiency.

Do you have definitions for the concepts centralized and decentralized?

I knew that other and smaller organizations had different structures and that shop size and configuration was not always related to organizational size or even number of donors. There are variations even within similar organizations of the same size. I have looked for inspiration from all types of organizations but have most often modeled our shop on similarly sized, decentralized public universities. Over time, the concept of a centralized versus decentralized organization has become simply an organizing principle for me and something I was in tune with as we developed programming for ADRP. I think the roles of staff, the types of programs and activities managed and the challenges faced differ along a spectrum from centralized to decentralized.

To me centralized means that there is one fundraising department and therefore one donor relations and stewardship shop in the organization; everyone is rowing in the same direction, according to the same plan. Everyone needn't be physically located in the same place, but one person or leadership team is setting the agenda. I believe that in a centralized configuration there is greater command and control of resources and the architecture of fundraising, including donor relations and stewardship. The approach is more rational when there is a central vision that tracks with the mission of the organization and holds the promise of a better overall donor experience.

Decentralized indicates that fundraising is divided among the units, divisions or programs. Different people or leadership teams are setting separate agendas; priorities may compete and are not as well organized according to their importance. In this situation, the approach to donors is generally less consistent and there is a greater sense of "ownership" over the donors at the unit level.

Perhaps you can see that I have a prejudice about which configuration provides more value to the donor and, thereby, the advancement program, at least at an organization of our size which functions with a decentralized model in many administrative functions. Given my exposure to so many different models, sizes and types of organizations, I fully appreciate that organizations can be more or less centralized or decentralized depending on leadership preferences of the organization's executives, fundraising cycles, and configuration and talents available in the units and divisions. I am well aware that there are plenty of well-qualified, highly successful professionals working in decentralized shops.

But centralization versus decentralization is not static; I see reorganization as a continuous process. The pendulum swings between centralized and decentralized as a function of what seems to be ideal for maximizing the donor experience and the fundraising outcome. From my perspective, the critical measure is whether the fundamental work of donor relations and stewardship—complying, acknowledging, recognizing, reporting, engaging—is being done and done well in terms of the donor's experience. If a new configuration will make the difference in the outcome, reorganization should be considered. If circumstances shift at the unit level, for instance, a new director or staff member with a different set of skills is hired, one might redistribute work back to the units.

There are triggers that let you know whether intervention or reorganization is in order. For instance, if acknowledgments are not being dispatched in a timely manner, this task might belong with a centralized team which has more resources and fewer distractions thereby hastening production. Outsourcing is another option that can be considered, especially for printing and mailing of reports, for example. Management of outside resources may be most efficiently managed from a centralized team, freeing the units to focus on customized content generation.

From my central position, I see opportunities to help with planning. For instance, we might suggest that the unit focus on the elements that are closest to the donor and likely to involve details specific to that unit, gift or donor. I'm thinking of acknowledgments, even if the tax receipt is centrally produced. A small-shop acknowledgment can be much more personal than one centrally produced. However, managing the selection of a building naming and the attendant signage may be better coordinated and organized from the central office.

Does shop size align with centralization vs. decentralization?

If we are talking only about these four concepts—large, small, centralized or decentralized—it is possible to say that the size and configuration of the institution will have a bearing on structure and size of the shops that support it. A large organization will probably have a central shop, usually with a large staff, providing foundational services for the departments or divisions that have their own advancement component, which is usually a staff of only one or two people. The extent to which the whole is centralized or decentralized depends on the leadership and priority- setting structure. In a smaller organization, a centralized shop of just one person may provide donor relations and stewardship services for the entire organization. In other words, while a large organization can have either a centralized or decentralized structure, a small organization will most likely have a centralized structure. That said, both size and centralization exist along a spectrum. The details differ from organization to organization and are likely to shift over time as needs change.

Have you identified typical characteristics along the two spectrums of shop size and centralization vs. decentralization?

Any large or central shop, even in a decentralized organization, must be more structured. Task specialization within the staff resources is typical. Larger operations often require more deliberation, even if they have more resources.

A small or a satellite operation in a decentralized environment typically has less structure and can operate in a more opportunistic manner. All small shops are more nimble and staff are usually generalists rather than specialists. One can do "this" right now and for just one donor. We also can't underestimate how much the support of technology has given us in loosening the structure of centralized shops.

The practitioner working in a small shop touches all aspects of donor service. Individual staff members are more likely to know something about fundraising and may be called in to provide another pair of eyes on any product or project. Almost by definition, truly small shops where one professional manages all donor relations and stewardship outcomes exist only when fundraising is centralized.

How can we tell what descriptors to apply within our own organizations? Is there a way to understand centralization/ decentralization and small/large in some coherent way, across all types of organizations?

The spectrum across which centralization/decentralization and small/ large operate is a matter of space and time as well. The organization of the shop and its size must serve a purpose, such as dealing with a particular point in the fundraising cycle or addressing a deficiency or resource constraint within a department. The central shop can help manage production while the satellites focus on managing donor relationships. The central operation can provide support during fundraising campaigns, taking on tasks that might ordinarily be managed in smaller, decentralized units.

Centralized versus decentralized; small versus large; these concepts seem set in stone. However, time and fundraising initiatives may require different approaches to providing excellent donor relations and stewardship services. Managers with responsibility for donor relations and stewardship must be vigilant about productivity and goal implementation. Reorganization, augmentation, and central support must be available when needed in order to ensure that the work of donor relations and stewardship is carried out.

Are you saying there is no definitive way to tell which concepts best describe the type of shop in which one works?

The question of how many management teams set the agenda resonates with me as the determiner of whether an organization is centralized or decentralized; the more management structure needed to plan, the more decentralized an organization is. Whether staff members are generalists or specialists seems to me to be the dividing line between small and large shops. The number of people and the reporting structure are secondary considerations.

Within different types of organizations, the way that people make sense of the complexity might vary. New employees must be helped to understand large, complex organizations and how their positions fit into the picture. Staff across an organization must have opportunities to engage leaders about emerging ideas and new directions and the leadership must figure out how to provide this level of communication.

In small shops, staff need to share ideas and discuss resource pooling or think about ways to satisfy some donor needs obliquely, taking advantage of opportunities outside the advancement office. We have to be aware as well that within an organization there may be divisions that look outside rather than inside for assistance. For example, a cancer center might look to the central advancement office within the medical center for advice and ideas, but a business school within a university might contact a peer in another institution for assistance.

The role of the leadership of the entire organization and especially the managers of donor relations and stewardship is to assess the needs of staff members to be prepared to do their best work. Bringing people together to discuss ideas and resources is the beginning and must be followed by integrating the results of these conversations to promote excellence. This type of reconnaissance helps determine whether a department must be reorganized or resources reallocated to support work in a satellite department.

What is the upside/downside of each model?

When I think about the advantages or disadvantages of centralized versus decentralized shops, I am concerned about the donor. To me, a centralized unit offers better coordination and a more consistent experience for the donors. For example, the centralized shop can better control the communication a donor receives. The donor is less likely to be bombarded with communications; the messages are less likely to be mixed and we can control the timing and volume of what goes in a donor's physical and virtual mail boxes. The downside of centralization is that, except for the donors at the top of the pyramid, engagement efforts may seem formulaic or repetitive.

In a decentralized or small shop, those providing donor relations and stewardship services are closer to the content that interests the donor. Part of the versatility of a small shop is the ability of staff members to reach out to other departments to provide content, to participate in engagement activities, to welcome donors and prospects when they visit. For small-shop staff, every day is likely to be different. For the right person, the need to interact across the organization keeps the work from becoming tedious or feeling isolated.

Small shops offer staff members greater professional opportunities to learn and do all aspects of donor relations and stewardship. These individuals become more well-rounded donor relations and stewardship professionals. Even so, the lack of bandwidth can wear down any donor relations and stewardship professional in a small shop. We all wish for more resources to do even the simplest things.

There can be virtue in that scarcity, however, because scarcity fosters innovation and creativity.

Finding staff who have experience in traditional donor relations and stewardship roles is challenging for all organizations. I'd like to recruit people with some background in the field so that I know that they are versed in the whys and wherefores of donor relations and stewardship practices; however, I have learned to appreciate enthusiasm, transferable skills, and a propensity for learning the nuances of donor relations over past experience.

Large shops are generally better resourced to develop long-standing programs, but they can become complacent if not forced to make tough decisions about how to allocate resources and stay aligned with what engages donors. It is important to avoid the temptation of "common practice" or "best practice" and truly seek "next practices" for your organization.

Technology can improve communication across a decentralized organization and/or large shop. Small shops benefit from consistent use of technology over a reliance on institutional memory or the skill of a single individual. At the same time, small shops must avoid purchasing software systems that don't communicate with institution-wide systems or that require upkeep and management that is eventually beyond the resources of a small shop.

For any configuration of these four concepts to be successful, there must be strong leadership and management. I believe that all the players must be encouraged to meet to work out their issues to provide the best donor experience and the most satisfying employee experience. This too takes leadership and strong management.

Are there requirements of donor relations and stewardship, no matter the structure or size of the shop?

I refer to the four elements defined by ADRP—gift acceptance and management, acknowledgment, donor recognition and reporting.

Those are the four requirements. Those objectives may be met by a combination of centralized or decentralized activities. The details are then specific to the choices made by the institution and its understanding of what best meets the needs of its donors.

What are the benefits of having specialists within donor relations and stewardship?

At UC Berkeley, I direct a central operation within a decentralized institution and I've come to see our work as providing a foundational level of stewardship upon which the units build, depending on their own resources and commitment to donor relations and stewardship. Originally, the stewardship team was a part of the advancement marketing and communications group at UC Berkeley. We've now changed this so that the work is more closely integrated with gift-management functions, so that we can better focus on the first element in the ADRP definition.

Another advantage of this change has to do with the differences between having a program and a project orientation. In my previous position at a bank, I noticed that the talents of the marketing and communications team is usually project driven. They understand how to bring a specific project to spectacular conclusion, but they don't necessarily plan for a next phase in the evolution of that outcome. Donor relations and stewardship professionals, however, appreciate the importance of building a program—a sustainable, versatile set of activities or outcomes that can be repeated over time. When we were part of the same organization it was challenging to make the case for resources to sustain programs versus resources for projects that launched campaigns, events, and websites.

What do you think are the ideal managerial characteristics of a leader in each type of organization?

The greatest challenge to any manager is to continuously improve the program so that people and programs don't get stale. It is important to strategize, prioritize and keep things fresh. Also, all leaders must manage up to introduce new ideas or changes in practice to the organization's leadership while providing an example to other staff, especially those without specific donor relations and stewardship training.

Managers in a large shop must keep specialized staff engaged and interested in what they are doing and give them opportunities to introduce new ideas. Managers in a larger or central shop in a decentralized organization must have extraordinary influencing skills in order to bring players across the institution along in accepting standards and guidelines. An important skill for the manager in this role is as a convener, to serve as an authority, an expert, someone who can help make decisions about donor relations and stewardship that benefit the entire organization.

In a small shop, the leader must be able to help others in the organization develop donor relations and stewardship skills, such as writing acknowledgments, telling the story of the organization or bringing a donor relations focus to an event. It is imperative that this manager learn to identify and rely on resources throughout the organization.

What skills are most important for a small, lightly resourced shop? What value does a large or centralized shop add to the organization?

Someone working in a small shop must be both analytical and creative. You have to have technical skills because you're going to have to manipulate data and make things look great on desktop software. You also have to make friends throughout the organization to find the resources—data, information, tips, help navigating politics, etc.—to get the job done.

The "center" provides a foundational level of donor relations and stewardship for all donors. In addition, the large, centralized shop can provide consultative support to small shops throughout the organization. UC Berkeley's office of donor and gift services is a large, central shop in a large, decentralized organization. I spend a lot of time walking around, finding out what's going on and how I can help promote the idea that having an office that understands donor relations and stewardship and can provide assistance and support is a good idea. We are always focused on the donor experience and that is the message that we spread in all interactions with colleagues.

A large shop can also convene all the shops across the organization to discuss what works and how to get things done. The central office can play a leadership role in defining standards, providing tools and systems, and can help rationalize the donor experience.

No matter what the configuration of your donor relations and stewardship program, individual units need to retain an entrepreneurial spirit about stewardship. The central, foundational team must encourage and empower units to have a person with donor relations and stewardship responsibilities to engage donors when any opportunity arises. This applies even in the tiniest of organizations; the service providers and subject experts must be inspired to contribute to maintaining a meaningful line of communication with donors.

It is always unwise for units or departments to purchase or create technology that will create shadow systems or other challenges to full integration with the central records-management system. Be cautious about mass-communication programs; donors do not want to receive multiple, unrelated communications, particularly solicitations. Donors want the institution to "know them" and to communicate according to their preferences and interests.

As technology evolves, there are certain tasks that benefit from specialized skill. For instance, mass customization and the coordinated use of social media require understanding of the tools and a talent for managing across the organization. These activities may be best managed from a centralized source, if for no other reason than to utilize the institution's resources in the most efficient way.

Thinking about these organizational models has been useful as I've built the donor relations and stewardship program at UC Berkeley, and evolved the organizational structure in which these activities occur. The key takeaway for me is that every institution has to define a structure that delivers the best donor experience possible, supports its fundraising objectives, and resonates with its leadership and administrative realities. Sometimes trade-offs will have to be made in terms of the level of centralization/decentralization, and the shop size might be driven by budgetary considerations more than anything else. The challenge, then, is to specify and execute a donor relations and stewardship program that is both affordable and effective. At the same time, the donor relations and stewardship professional should always be thinking about what she believes things should look like on a distant horizon when the value of her work is above reproach and resources are more plentiful. If she is poised to take advantage of that, she can use these organizational models to guide both incremental and transformational changes.

Nancy Lubich McKinney is the executive director of Donor and Gift Services at University of California, Berkeley. She is the author of "Stewardship in a Decentralized Fundraising Environment," in *Intentional Stewardship: Bringing Your Donors to Their Highest Level of Philanthropy*. She is a long-standing member of the Association of Donor Relations Professionals and served as President of that organization 2009-2014.

Appendix 1: Donor Bill of Rights

Philanthropy is based on voluntary action for the common good. It is a tradition of giving and sharing that is primary to the quality of life. To assure that philanthropy merits the respect and trust of the general public, and that donors and prospective donors can have full confidence in the not-for-profit organizations and causes they are asked to support, we declare that all donors have these rights:

1. To be informed of the organization's mission, of the way the organization intends to use donated resources, and of its capacity to use donations effectively for their intended purposes.
2. To be informed of the identity of those serving on the organization's governing board, and to expect the board to exercise prudent judgment in its stewardship responsibilities.
3. To have access to the organization's most recent financial statements.
4. To be assured their gifts will be used for the purposes for which they were given.
5. To receive appropriate acknowledgment and recognition.
6. To be assured that information about their donations is handled with respect and with confidentiality to the extent provided by law.
7. To expect that all relationships with individuals representing organizations of interest to the donor will be professional in nature.
8. To be informed whether those seeking donations are volunteers, employees of the organization or hired solicitors.
9. To have the opportunity for their names to be deleted from mailing lists that an organization may intend to share.
10. To feel free to ask questions when making a donation and to receive prompt, truthful and forthright answers.

Appendix 2: Donor Relations and Stewardship Defined

Donor relations is the comprehensive effort of any nonprofit that seeks philanthropic support to ensure that donors experience high-quality interactions with the organization that foster long-term engagement and investment. This effort is commonly thought to have four elements.

The first, *gift acceptance and management*, encompasses policies and procedures that address a variety of issues that must be considered before accepting gifts, as well as procedures that ensure that gifts are put to work as donors intend. Among these are:

- Processes for reviewing gifts to ensure that the donor's intentions and the organizations needs are congruous. Having an up-front understanding of whether or not a gift can be deployed according to the donor's wishes can mitigate a loss of goodwill and, possibly, the need to return a gift in the future.

- Structures for giving opportunities, including the levels required to establish endowed funds, or to be recognized with named spaces, on donor walls or in giving societies.

- Procedures for tracking the expenditure of gifts to ensure that they are being used according to donors' intentions, and mechanisms for rectifying situations where they are not. Importantly, organizations need to have processes for handling gifts that can no longer be utilized because of changes in programming or external factors such as changes in laws. These processes need to address instances where the donor is living as well as those where the donor is deceased.

The second element, ***acknowledgment***, covers the protocols for
and execution of accurate, timely, and meaningful expressions of
gratitude. Acknowledgement is a private action directed by the
organization to the donor. It includes both gift receipting, which
addresses the requirements of the Internal Revenue Service, and
personalized, written correspondence. It might also include emails,
phone calls, and visits. In most cases, the most heartfelt and impactful
acknowledgements come from those who directly benefit from a
donor's generosity—for example, clients of a social services agency,
artists of a performing arts company, or students of a college or
university.

Donor recognition is the third element, and, importantly, includes
donor recognition ***events***. This element incorporates opportunities
and mechanisms for meaningful donor recognition, taking into
consideration such factors as donors' preferences (for example,
anonymity and the format in which their names are presented) and
institutional culture and values. Recognition is the public form of
donor acknowledgement, and ranges from activities that are automatic
organizational responses to giving, such as giving societies, to those
that are undertaken with the involvement of the donors, as is the case
with named space signage. Examples of recognition programs include:

- ***Giving societies*** and ***honor rolls*** categorize donors according to
  their levels of giving. Depending on how they are structured, they
  may reflect only a certain type of giving—for example, giving to
  annual funds only, to certain areas of the organization, or during
  a specified period of time, such as during a campaign—or may be
  defined to be cash-based or to include pledges to give in the future.
  The treatment of particular forms of giving, such as deferred or
  planned gifts, and gifts-in-kind, must also be determined when
  giving society and honor roll programs are developed.

  Giving societies often incorporate tiers that incent donors to reach
  to higher levels of giving. The tiers are generally named and may
  offer differential benefits or courtesies. For some organizations
  it is appropriate for the benefits to have tangible value, which
  then impacts the tax deductibility of gifts as stipulated by the

Internal Revenue Service. It is increasingly common, however, for such benefits to offer access to the content and leadership of the organization, thereby mitigating the quid-pro-quo issues that organizations must manage.

Honor rolls also categorize donors according to levels of giving and are usually incorporated into print publications, such as campaign progress reports and annual reports, to signal the specific contributions of individual and organizational donors in the context of the total raised. While most donors will say that they do not require this form of recognition, many will be candid about the fact that it's of interest to see where they stack-up in relation to other supporters. This type of friendly competition can be a very useful tool in fundraising. The preparation of honor rolls can be tedious, and they must be checked multiple times to assure that they are error free. The ability to make changes as necessary, as well as cost savings offered, are strong reasons to move the delivery of honor rolls from print to online. This, in fact, is a very frequent topic of best practice research. This decision, however, must take into account the potential impact on donors, particularly those giving at major and principal gift levels, and must be in-line with the overall communication strategy of the organization.

- **Donor walls** and **named space signage** provide very visible recognition, usually for those giving to campaigns and capital projects. Donor walls can also be used to recognize annual and lifelong giving. It is critical to define standards for listings, and to confirm those standards with internal decision-makers, before approaching donors about listing options.

A very important consideration for both types of physical recognition is the handling of the removal of walls and signage when spaces are re-purposed or demolished. Organizations should have policies for dealing with these situations, and should communicate early with donors, or heirs of donors, who will be affected.

- *Donor profiles* in publications such as newsletters, magazines and annual reports, as well as their online counterparts, and *external publicity* such as press releases, are also very public forms of recognition. Donors or their representatives should be actively involved in the preparation and review of these materials to mitigate potentially embarrassing errors or omissions.

- *Donor recognition events, awards, mementos* and *volunteer engagement opportunities* are also important forms of donor recognition. They can be features of giving societies, annual funds, and campaigns, or can stand-alone as opportunities to engage and cultivate donors as they move toward their next gifts.

  Events have a prominent place in the donor relations toolkit because they are an effective way to reach and foster long-term relationships with a broad spectrum of donors. As such, they are often the focal point of the work of donor relations professionals, and can range from large-scale events where the objective is to create and reinforce connection, to intimate gatherings that deepen personal relationships between the organization's leadership and its most important donors.

The final element is *reporting* to donors on the impact of their gifts on the mission of the organization. This involves standards, systems and methods of delivery for demonstrating fiscal accountability—prudent investment and spending in accordance with donors' expectations—to donors, to convey ongoing appreciation, and to report on the impact of philanthropic support. Reporting falls into two broad categories: 1) qualitative, which is the storytelling that confirms to the donor that the investment was a sound one because the support is making a difference in the mission of the organization, and 2) quantitative, which verifies the carrying-out of fiduciary responsibility. Further, reporting can be included in print and online vehicles that are broadly distributed, or can be highly personalized. The latter can range from simple financial reports regarding the status of an endowed fund to comprehensive philanthropy impact reports that chronicle several decades of investment in the organization. Information technology tools are providing opportunities to "mass-customize" reports, so that each follows the same templated format but includes donor-specific data.

It is common today for this element to be referred to as *stewardship*. This word, however, has been defined historically as the safeguarding of the assets of others and, therefore, is considered by some to be misused in the context of donors, as in "donor stewardship." Rather, these individuals state that it is gifts, not donors, that are stewarded. In this view, the activities associated with stewardship are focused on ensuring that the funds provided by donors are utilized in the way intended as conveyed in gift agreements and fund terms. By this definition, stewardship is a function inherently internal to an organization, rather than a donor-facing, external function.

Those who subscribe to a broader definition of stewardship, and who are comfortable with the use of the phrase "donor stewardship," are, however, clear in the understanding that while all stewardship is donor relations, not all donor relations is stewardship.

The field of donor relations has grown, in part, as a response to the greater sophistication of donors as informed philanthropists and their increasing scrutiny of the outcomes of the organizations they fund. This has necessitated more reporting which has the potential to uncover organizational weaknesses in terms of spending donations in the manner intended. This is not due to ill intent but, rather, to the inability to track the numerous documents and the clauses they contain in any kind of systematic fashion. Advances in information technology have certainly improved the situation, but, in the meantime, many organizations have implemented "donor stewardship" activities that take an externally-oriented view of bringing donors closer to the outcomes they are making possible, thereby demonstrating that the organization is indeed fulfilling its fiduciary responsibility to deploy the funding as the donor intended. In fact, in many organizations the terms donor relations and stewardship are now used interchangeably.

The use of these terms and the activities that comprise a specific donor relations or stewardship professional's responsibilities are often driven by the organization's structure and where these people are situated on the proverbial organizational chart. These responsibilities can variously be in the operational, financial, communications, or fundraising or "development" areas. There is no one best practice approach to defining the donor relations role, but the following are general observations regarding how these roles are defined based on organizational structures:

- Not surprisingly, there is more specialization in larger organizations, whereas donor relations professionals in small organizations tend to be in "one stop" shops.

- Gift acceptance and management is generally part of the donor relations role when donor relations is part of operations, and not part of the role when donor relations is aligned with communications.

- Responsibility for events can be separate from donor relations in very large organizations.

- Management of giving societies is often part of the role of the annual fund team, rather than the donor relations team.

- Donor relations and stewardship are sometimes separated into different functions, with donor relations being part of fundraising or communications, and stewardship being aligned with operations or finance.

Wherever the donor relations function is placed in the organization, and irrespective of the specific portfolio of responsibilities for which it is responsible, a crucial factor in its success is the partnerships forged with other areas and functions. Strong internal relationships with other development disciplines such as planned giving, principal and major giving, and prospect research, as well as functions such as finance and the actual philanthropic beneficiaries, are key to ensuring that the organization puts its best face forward to the donor. Partnerships with vendors enable donor relations work and can, if vendors are used repeatedly, extend the reach of staff in building long-term relationships with donors. The most important partnership, though, is that developed with the donors themselves, because well-tended long-term relationships produce effective ambassadors, stewards, and peer-to-peer fundraisers.

In implementing or evolving a donor relations effort it is useful to note that donor relations and stewardship activities should be proactive but can be organized according to donor actions that fall broadly into five categories, as follows:

- The first is *transactional*, which refers to the arrival of a gift or pledge (a new commitment). Pledge payments and matching gifts are also transactional, though they may not elicit the same response from the institution.

- *Annual giving*, the second category of donor activity, is often associated with giving societies.

- The third category of donor activity is *lifetime giving*, which can also be associated with giving societies. It is important to note that a first gift should be considered a first step toward reaching a lifetime giving milestone.

- The fourth category, *deferred giving*, depends on the sophistication of the gift planning options the organization extends to prospects, as well as its fundraising priorities. If an organization does offer an array of vehicles, decisions should be made in terms of how each will "count" toward giving totals, giving societies, and honor rolls. Importantly, these activities should differentiate gift intentions from irrevocable planned gifts.

- The final category of donor activity concerns the gift designation— *endowment versus current use versus capital project*. In other words, is the gift supporting people, programs or buildings? In many cases this last category will, during a capital or comprehensive campaign, align with specific fundraising themes or goals.

59967651R00080

Made in the USA
Charleston, SC
20 August 2016